2009 Poetry C

I have a dream 2009

Words to change the world

Martin Luther King

John Lennon

Verses From The West Midlands

Edited by Donna Samworth

First published in Great Britain in 2009 by:

 Young**Writers**

Young Writers
Remus House
Coltsfoot Drive
Peterborough
PE2 9JX
Telephone: 01733 890066
Website: www.youngwriters.co.uk

Foreword

'I Have a Dream 2009' is a series of poetry collections written by 11 to 18-year-olds from schools and colleges across the UK and overseas. Pupils were invited to send us their poems using the theme 'I Have a Dream'. Selected entries range from dreams they've experienced to childhood fantasies of stardom and wealth, through to inspirational poems of their dreams for a better future and of people who have influenced and inspired their lives.

The series is a snapshot of who and what inspires, influences and enthuses young adults of today. It shows an insight into their hopes, dreams and aspirations of the future and displays how their dreams are an escape from the pressures of today's modern life. Young Writers are proud to present this anthology, which is truly inspired and sure to be an inspiration to all who read it.

Contents

The Poems

I Have A Dream

Out of the hustle, out of the city,
Please find me somewhere that's peaceful and pretty.
Work? I'll work harder - I know I can make it!
People and pavements - I've just got to shake it.
Terms will fly by like the views from the track,
Head down to laptop and clickety-clack.
Fly through the finals with turmoil and anguish;
Don't let me fail - if I fail I will languish!
Give me, deserving, that precious diploma,
Grateful and gasping, I'll breathe now it's over.

And now . . . breathe deep . . .
Slowing down, down;
Turning around, round, round . . .
To appreciate fully the wonder of what
I beseechingly hope to have found . . .

My farmhouse sits, quiet and content,
Like a frog in a pond, nestled and cupped in its valley,
A jewel in the Emerald Isle.
Sheep shout in broad brogue
And cows crunch contentedly, brewing butter for local markets.
Horses gleam like conkers in autumn, with foals that stagger in like spring.
Dogs cluster at my heels and
No one cares what I wear, or how I do my hair.

Send me the knowledge to tend my stock
And the strength to weather adversity.
Send me the focus to work for my dream;
(And the money for university!)

Tori Pearson (16)
Belvidere School, Shrewsbury

1

The Wonderful World

I observe the morning sky
Over a cup of creamy coffee
And I see several gardeners
Mowing the grounds for me
My mind is at peace and everything is perfect

Oh, what a wonderful world we live in.

My morning starts with the ringing of a bell
I kicked off my duvet and off the bed I fell
My clothes are in the wardrobe
A vast selection there
I brushed my teeth and combed my hair

Oh what a wonderful world we live in.

I stare out of a dirt-spattered window
And I see a world of suffering, poverty and neglect
A man limping on one leg
A woman scavenging for scraps
And a baby abandoned on a sidewalk

Oh what a wonderful world we live in.

I squinted up at the dark night's sky
From my cardboard box, all damp and drear
My stomach is rumbling, there's no food here
And my family is lost
To the terrible cost . . .
I'm all alone in my little cardboard box

Oh what a wonderful world we live in.

Alice Scoggins & Cara Fairley (16)
Belvidere School, Shrewsbury

Ode To Roger Moore

Where art thou thy Bond?
You have disappeared from our screens
We are so fond,
It is long since you have been
Where art thou thy Bond?

Tonight I sat up late,
Watching Moonraker again,
It left me in such a state,
I ate some chicken chow mein,
And then I dropped the plate.

When will you return?
Fans are awaiting,
I think I'm going to burn,
Inside I am baking.
When will you return?

Age is a virtue
Death will come
You are due,
So have some fun
Merci beaucoup.

Legend is a tough word,
Too few qualify,
But like a bird
You live to fly,
Are you the spy who loved me?

Alex Gibbons (16)
Belvidere School, Shrewsbury

Ode To Roger Moore

Where art thou thy Bond?
You have disappeared from our screens
We are so fond,
It is long since you have been
Where art thou thy Bond?

Tonight I sat up late,
Watching Moonraker again,
It left me in such a state,
I ate some chicken chow mien,
And then I dropped the plate.

When will you return?
Fans are awaiting,
I think I'm going to burn,
Inside I am baking.
When will you return?

Age is a virtue
Death will come
You are due,
So have some fun
Merci beaucoup.

Legend is a tough word,
Too few qualify,
But like a bird
You live to fly,
Are you the spy who loved me?

Owen Witherow (15)
Belvidere School, Shrewsbury

Save The Earth

Why do you have to drive to work?
It makes you look like a berk
Ride your bike
I'm sure you'll like
You can lose all your weight
And save the fate
Of the Earth.

The ice caps are melting
The world is smelting
You don't want to make the world die
As we will all cry
The Earth is our home
And now it's all alone
Save the Earth.

The animals will disappear
It's what we all fear
The gibbons will go
Because we were too slow
To save the Earth!

Daniel Jones (15) & Andrew Hodson (17)
Belvidere School, Shrewsbury

Stop, Stare And Take A Minute

Stop, stare and take a minute
To sit and watch the world go by

Is this all we'll ever know?
Happiness and peace, all one lie

Stop, stare and take a minute
To sit and watch the world go by

We fight a war with ourselves
Awarding men with medals, why?

Stop, stare and take a minute
To sit and watch the world go by

Spend savings on useless stuff . . .
People sit alone, left to die.

So stop, stare and take a minute
To think about all the things we're missing.

Sofie Linney (16)
Belvidere School, Shrewsbury

Justice And Judgement

Justice and judgement, two words of a kind,
They rule human nature, infect human minds,
Laws, lords and ladies, oblivious with power,
Destroying humanity, watch their poison flower,

To judge by a cover is a disgrace to all taste,
Make rights for human nature; don't hate the human race,
Segregate your souls, and keep civil power sedated,
Listen to the government to let war be elevated,

Your mind is your own; don't let them make your choice,
Anyone with a brain can shout out their voice,
They educate and evaluate for bombs of full precision,
So listen to this, give death a kiss and make your own decision,

Power is just an excuse; no man can promote war,
Madmen, sick with blood, cut up the world with saws.

Arthur Mellor (16)
Belvidere School, Shrewsbury

United Together

United together we can fight crime,
United together we can do it in time,
Together we can.

United together we can stop this war,
United together we can help the poor,
Together we can.

United together we can prevent CO_2 gases,
United together we can do it in the masses,
Together we can.

United together we can battle cancer,
United together we can find an answer,
Together we can.

We have a dream, together we can.

Charlotte Moazami (15) & Steph Langford-Perry (16)
Belvidere School, Shrewsbury

My Dream

My dream is for everyone to have money
People deserve money
Money is the key to health
Money is what we need.

People deserve food
Food is the key to keep healthy
Food is what we need.

People deserve clothes
Clothes are what we need to keep us covered,
Clothes are what keep us warm.

This world needs to be fair,
Equal these items out fairly.

Scott Oddy (12)
Caludon Castle School, Coventry

Whose War?

We argue over religion
We argue over debt
We disagree about culture
We blackmail and we threat.

We listen to the government
We place our trust in them
We fight the war that they declared
We vote them in again.

We are the innocent in this warfare
This war's not ours to fight
It's between the leaders of our country
Some don't know wrong from right.

We are the children who are bleeding
We've lost loved ones dear
Who fought for the country
While the culprits hide in fear.

My dream is that democracy
Will triumph over all
This war is not our children's
But they're the ones who fall.

We want a better future
Without warfare, without strife
Can't we overcome our differences
And live peaceful, happy lives?

Laura Gaffney (13)
Caludon Castle School, Coventry

I Have A Dream

I have a dream
For the world to be peaceful
For the people to be kind
For everyone to be equal.

I have a dream
For the bullying to stop
For the world to be on top
For the people to be loving.

I have a dream
For the war to end
To stop the fighting
For everyone to be friends.

I have a dream
For the racism to stop
For people to accept people for who they are
For everyone to be loving.

I have a dream
For everyone to be happy
For everyone to be kind
For everyone to be family.

I have a dream . . .
I have a dream . . .
I have a dream . . .

Rajvir Bachu (12)
Caludon Castle School, Coventry

My Dream . . .

I have a dream, that is to help the poor,
Who don't even have a bed
And who have to sleep on the floor.
I have a dream, that is to help the less fortunate
And give them food and education
And let them have a better future than me.
I have a dream, which is to be a millionaire,
And then explore the unknown
And discover things that no one has ever discovered before.
I have a dream, that is to stop child abuse
And let kids live their own life
And let them have their own aspirations and let it come true.
I have a dream, which is to build a children's home
With my very own hands
And bring the children without a home in.
I have a dream, that is to stop animal cruelty
And save the 'soon to be extinct'.
I have a dream, that is to be the world's best and smartest genius in
mathematics, who can solve any equation and sum.
I have a dream, which is to stop terrorism
And bring peace to Earth and stop wars and cultures
Colliding into each other, making it even harder to stop.
I have a dream which is to live the dreams that I want.

Jaskaran Sembi (11)
Caludon Castle School, Coventry

My Dream Poem

I have a dream
Where the land is clean
Everybody is equal
Hate should not be a sequel.

There was once a time
When the world was divided
And black and white
Were fighting for civil rights.

Now everyone's accepted
And everyone is friends
But we cannot forget
What people never tried to mend.

Now I have a dream
That someday the world will
Be happy and peaceful
And not have to be regretful.

George Wills (13)
Caludon Castle School, Coventry

My World Inspiration

Fighting on the battlefields
Fighting on the beaches
Shouting to our soldiers
Long, loud preaches,
Without blood, death or decay
The enemy will pay
With our loyal gracious Queen
The world can be green,
So get an inspiration
Maybe friends, family or love,
Sitting in the window
Watching a hummingbird or a dove,
So get some friends and family,
Get someone to hug,
Do not turn out with a bad life
And do not be a mug.
I have an inspiration
My family and their love
So all you have to say
Is please give me a shove.

Who's your inspiration?

Ethan Piggott (12)
Caludon Castle School, Coventry

I Have A Dream

I have a dream
To change the world,
To stop racism,
And bring world peace.

I have a dream
To save the world,
Enough with wars,
We need harmony.

I have a dream,
When we are all the same,
But unique and different,
In our own special way.

I have a dream
To change the world,
When we can all be together,
Us not them.

Ellie Ashley (11)
Caludon Castle School, Coventry

I Have A Dream

I have a dream
That poverty will end
And peace will start
That the hunger of the Earth will be filled.

I have a dream
That the drought of Africa will be quenched,
And that the dreams of the poor
Will be made reality.

I have a dream!
I have a dream!
I have a dream!

Amy Chaston (11)
Caludon Castle School, Coventry

14

I Have A Dream!

I am really excited,
For the whole world to be united
No hatred, no war,
No people being so poor.

I want a world,
So free of crime
No killing, no stealing,
A perfect world for the rest of time.

I have a vision,
Of a world full of light
No fighting, no anger,
Everything to be just right.

Together we are the human race,
Let's treat our world with airs and grace
Together we'll work as a team,
So now I can fulfil my dream.

Hafsah Habib (12)
Caludon Castle School, Coventry

I Wish . . .

I wish that there were no more wars,
And that we could just close the doors.
I wish that everyone could be equal,
We can all be good people.
I wish the times could change.

I wish that all of the bullying would stop,
We need the bullying chain to drop.
I wish the hatred would end,
Everyone should have a friend.
I wish the times could change.

Lydia Herron (13)
Caludon Castle School, Coventry

My Dream For The Future

My dream for the future
I'd like it to be
A peaceful world
For you and me.

No hating people
No being mean
No dropping litter
To keep the country clean.

Find a cure for all diseases
So people can live a healthy life
No murders committed again
Especially no crimes involving a knife.

As you can see
I would like the future to be
A happy place for you and me.

Sarah Johnson (12)
Caludon Castle School, Coventry

It Hasn't Got A Name

The world I want is quite imaginary,
Clean air and unpolluted sea,
Dirty puffs of air will no longer exist,
These are just some on my very long list.

Purple, mottled bruises caused by abuse,
Why can't people cut the anger loose?
Fuming, sore knuckles and crashing into cars,
Do you regret it now you're behind bars?

Your heart has been held together by Sellotape,
Your family torn apart from this like rape.
Pieces of your heart falling off each day,
Until you are left with nothing to say.

A racist is what people fear to be called,
Teasing someone for their colour,
And their world suddenly gets duller.

Emily Dixon (11)
Caludon Castle School, Coventry

Dreams

When the day comes . . .
Problems will be solved
Unhappiness will serve with a smile
Arson burnt to cinders
Violence is murdered
Criminals behind bars
Feeling low soars through the clouds
Feeling blue warmed up
Bullying scared away
War shot down
Dreams all over the world
The world was shared evenly
Among us all.

Christopher Taylor (11)
Etone College, Nuneaton

17

Band Of Brothers

Dropping,
Static lines pulling chutes,

Dropping,
Rifle clicks and crunching boots,

Dropping,
Leaders lost and leaders found,

Dropping,
Blithe in his foxhole, in the ground,

Dropping,
Replacements really not fitting in,

Dropping,
Eindhoven causing quite a din,

Dropping,
Winter's writing out reports,

Dropping,
Winter's lost in heavy thoughts,

Dropping,
In Bastogne, a medic in a hut,

Dropping,
The reply to the Germans is 'nut's,

Dropping,
Compton, Muck, Penkala, destroyed,

Dropping,
Dike wimps out in the attack on Foy,

Dropping,
Easy still in the snow,

Dropping,
Capturing prisoners, you know,

Easy company knew that when things got bad
They could always rely on each other.

Dougie Stilgoe (12)
Etone College, Nuneaton

Gangster's Story

Imagine
Being uncomfortable in your own house,
Imagine
Walking outside and getting shot,
Imagine
Killing someone just for the name,
Imagine
Having to rat out your own blood,
Imagine
Feeling redemption all your life,
Imagine
Being able to trust no one, not even yourself,
Imagine
Buying a bullet and knowing its fate.

What if
The light shows another path?
What if
Another gun is never bought?
What if
Another bullet is never used?
What if
There is a hidden doorway away from the cesspit of life?
What if
Cars are bought not stolen?
What if
Families did not have to weep for the murdered?
What if
You were able to trust everyone?

This is the gangster's story and it has to *stop!*

This is the children's story and it has to *stop!*

Hamza Bham (11)
Etone College, Nuneaton

19

One Day

Is there any hope? Is there?
There is always hope, however small.
Wars shall one day be forgotten,
They shall just be faint whispers on the wind,
A small pebble falling from a hilltop.
But now we must fight,
So peace shall one day return,
So our children's children
And their children's children shall live in harmony.
Money will not be wasted on war, arson or murders,
But on medicines, technology or discovery.
Man shall be someone to turn to.
Love will be the new war,
Hope, the guns that we now have grasped in our hands!
But most of all peace . . .
Shall be the greater version of all things.
Evil and cruel, bullying and wars.

One day
When the sun
Shines
That little bit
Brighter
That shall be
A day
To remember,
Peace shall
Once more
Settle
Upon the
Land!

Jamie Downs (12)
Etone College, Nuneaton

Rejection

Rejection, something that happens all the time,
Kids being tortured to get them to leave school.
Rejection, deception, some have to be so passive,
So forgiving every day.

Every day unimaginable chaos taken out
On the innocent people.
Glue-sticks, pens, pencils, pencil cases all thrown about,
But when the teacher turns around, evil hides,
Nothing wrong, no pencils on the floor,
No noise, no anything.
Only there are the trouble-makers, who hide the chaos,
The hidden bruises, the hidden pain, hidden mess.
How? How, I say, does it disappear?
Oh no, the teacher's turning to the board,
Here we go again,
Chaos, once again, reigns supreme.

Sometimes I want to *charge* at some certain people,
Sometimes I just want to *roar*,
There is a choice, bullying or peace,
Why do it when there are inconsiderable, terrible consequences ahead of
that path?
Why do it? Entertainment? Respect? Pleasure?
There is no proper reason or excuse
For such heart-breaking actions,
Or to demolish someone's feelings.

So much frustration, power, revenge,
I just want bullying to stop.
Why do it . . . ? Now, please, just cease the pain.

Sam Johnston (12)
Etone College, Nuneaton

21

Don't Be Cruel To Animals

Animals are cute
Animals are cuddly
But you would not like it
If they were extinct.

Hunting is wrong
Hunting is bad
Don't be caught doing it
Or you'll be sad.

Donate money
To help the animals
Make your pets
As happy as possible.

Don't be cruel to pets
If otherwise
You will regret.

Pets are your responsibility
If something happened to them
You'll never forgive yourself.

It is cruel to keep animals in cages
So let the animals be free.

Animals are sad
Animals are unhappy
But if you helped one they'll be glad.

People are mean
People are cruel
They are so bad to the animals.

Michael Clarke (12)
Etone College, Nuneaton

Untitled

The sun was setting over
A quiet sea,
The wind had dropped and
The gulls were free,

I dozed and dreamt
Of days of yore
When I was a child
Oh how I adore,

The summers then were
Long and hot
And the sun would glow
Like a fiery dot,

I remember those days
When the fair came to town
And just riding the Ferris wheel
Would lift my frown,

Candyfloss in sugary wisps
Is my idea of heavenly bliss,

The smell of the sea
Would fill my nose
And grains of sand
Would tickle my toes,

And running far
To reach the shore
In my dreams
I'm there once more.

Keira Barr (14)
Etone College, Nuneaton

The Devastation Of Cancer

It can be devastating when you know you have got it,
You can get it when you smoke.
It can get more and more if you smoke,
You can get it anywhere in your body,
When you get it you get weaker and weaker every weekend.

If you get cancer you will lose your hair,
You can give money if you care.
If you are lucky you can get surgery,
You get skinnier,
You go hollow in the body,
You might get wrinkly on the skin.

You can see the history of cancer on me,
Cancer is black,
You can be born with it or die with it,
You can get it in the young age or the old age,
It does not matter, so check it out soon.
It's not about the look it's about the soul,
You can go away or stay, stay, stay.

Please get better but have hope so it will get better,
It might be a fight but do it till the light,
Come on, you can make it, you know life is shaky,
But it is a good opportunity.
It might be discussed but it is worth a bit of a hit,
You will make it,
You have to get a whiff of this,
You might cry but try,
You need to help so get some family help.

Harry Forman (12)
Etone College, Nuneaton

Dream

It's in your imagination,
It's in, your head,
It might be what you want,
It might be of your deathbed,
Maybe for the future,
Maybe about the past,
Maybe full of fear,
Maybe full of lies,
Possibly the truth,
They are all you dreams.

It could be of power,
Maybe of impossible feats,
It might be like normal life,
It may be great evil,
Nightmares as they're known,
Maybe destruction,
Maybe failure,
Maybe death,
They are just dreams.

It could be at night,
It could be by day,
It could be your future,
It could be your destiny,
Maybe kindnesses will show,
Maybe darkness will prevail,
Will our dreams ever fail?

Matthew Stevens (12)
Etone College, Nuneaton

Death Stalks The Land

Hate flourishes deep in the hearts of the soldiers
Torn from families - knowing they may never return,
Forced to fight to prevent oppression of families,
Death stalks the land.

Over the top and into no-man's-land,
Dressed in a redcoat with a sword in your hand.
The waiting is over, the battle's begun,
Death stalks the land.

Messerschmitts, Spitfires drop bombs on the land
Spreading discord, destruction, death among men.
Farmers come soldiers, war turns friend against friend,
And once more - death stalks the land.

Families weep - bereaved for their lost ones,
Woe grips their hearts - why won't these wars stop?
Battalions of soldiers lie six feet under
Death has taken its toll.

Yet the families are thankful - pleased for their safety,
Grateful for the protection that was given in blood,
Some warriors return home, all bedecked with medals
And slowly peace takes its hold on the land.

Poppies grow upwards - newly awoken
Remembrance of the wars that have been.
Prevent these wars so no more may fall,
So death will ne'er again stalk the land.

Toby Melville (12)
Etone College, Nuneaton

AVFC Stars

Ashley Young romps down the wing
With a bit of a swagger and swing,
He's up and down and everywhere
Like a roller coaster ride that's at the fair.

Then the ball gets put in the box
And there's John Carew, who's there like a fox
And there's John Carew playing the game.

With Martin Laursen, no longer there,
Our defence is not impregnable, so some teams say,
We're bound to struggle this season
But the Villa say that that's no reason
As Martin O'Neill will surely bag another centre-half.

Then there's Stiliyan Petrov,
Who keeps the midfield together,
No one gets past the mighty Stan Petrov
'Cause his strength is as strong as leather.

Now for Gareth Barry, who has been predicted to leave,
Although the Villa fans will almost certainly grieve,
We'll bring in another star
With potential to be great for the future.

Now for the gaffer, Martin O'Neill,
Who at the Villa we strongly feel,
He will break us into the elite top 4,
And for the defensive deal in the summer we'll find a cure.

Callum Allen (12)
Etone College, Nuneaton

The Racism Rap

I'm waiting for the day
Where it will come,
When the racism will
Be finished and done.

I'm waiting for the day,
When we will be the same,
So stop this nonsense and
Stop this game.

I'm waiting for the day
When people stop taking
The Mick, because it's
Never getting old but it
Is still sick.

I'm waiting for the day,
When people are, I just
Want people to see what I
See.

I'm waiting for the day
When they will stop,
Maybe one day something in their head
Will pop.

I can't wait for this day
To come, but they don't want
To stop, according to some.

Harry Arnthal (12)
Etone College, Nuneaton

War Is Here . . .

Run to the nearest shelter,
Hear the ringing of the siren,
The roaring and rumbling of the aeroplanes,
All the distress it's causing.

Keep quiet, don't move,
Or else the planes might see us,
Their job is to bomb our entire place,
When will this war end?

Imagine the peace at the end,
All the distress gone
Our families reunited,
We are all back again as one.

See the army at the end,
March back into town,
Loved ones run to each other,
And children cry.

How good you feel to be a family,
All back to normal,
But all the time you have to fight for the country,
So more wars you will do.

Soon off he goes to fight again,
But begging him not to go,
He hugs you goodbye and leaves,
To fight yet another war.

Daisy Horsfall (12)
Etone College, Nuneaton

What's Wrong With The World?

What's wrong with the world?
Racism.
Why? We are all a family,
We are all the same inside,
Sure we don't look the same,
Sure we might not share interests,
But why do we have to fight?
What is it with wars?
Wars, death, why is it all there?
Why do we put up with this?
Put up with the destruction of our countries,
Our planet,
Put up with vandalism,
The ruining of our world.
Disgraceful dirt, graffiti.
What sort of people do this?
Sick-minded people growing in our world.
But there is hope,
We can change people,
Help people,
Stop them while we can,
Help not only ourselves,
But others.
There is more than disappointment and sadness . . .
There is hope.

Fraser Bircher (11)
Etone College, Nuneaton

War

Close the history books
And make war history.
Make it the past.
Drop our weapons and don't fight back . . .

Joseph Grant (11)
Etone College, Nuneaton

You DO Have A Voice, You DO Have A Choice

In war you don't have a choice,
In war you don't have a voice.

Why does everyone have to fight?
It's as if they believe it's alright.
We are forced like machines to go to battle,
Unable to just evade the thunderous rattle.

I thought the slavery age had expired,
But apparently not, as in some opinions we are not admired.
The possibility of death is very high,
And everyone is expecting the end to be nigh.

Crowds may try to halt a war,
Preventing deaths and suffering injuries no more.
Shouldn't the government interfere?
The people concerned want to conclude the tears.

Getting behind them we can put the gun down to redeem,
Then shake the hand of the opposing team.
To send a message to everyone, doesn't matter your name,
We're all equal and we're all the same!

In war you *do* have a voice,
In war you *do* have a choice.

Ryan Farndon (12)
Etone College, Nuneaton

I Have A Dream!

I have a dream that I will be famous,
I have a dream that I will be a superstar!
But the most I dream about is being with my friends.

Molly Smith (12)
Etone College, Nuneaton

31

Smoking

I dream to say
Goodbye to the
Fog that lives
Inside and outside
My body.

Why pay so much
When you can pay
The rent?

Think of the victim
Around you when
You light it up.

What's the point, paying to die
When you've got a life
Ahead of you?

Why don't you stop to
Help others?

I have a dream to
Stop people killing themselves.

This is how to stop smoking
Ring the NHS
And get a non-smoking pack.

Luke Randle (11)
Etone College, Nuneaton

I Have A Dream!

I have a dream that one day
I will have friends.
I have a dream that one day people will
Stop bullying me!
But the most I dream about is . . .
Being myself!

Abbi Baldwin (12)
Etone College, Nuneaton

Sorphinbuski

Things would be swell and easy if there
Was one word to change the world
With the roll of a tongue
In the blink of a tired eye
All would be well and fair

Pain and fear washed away in the tide
Of a magical miracle word
The tragedies and sorrows caused by
The gun and the fist and the sword
If hurts were healed and wrongs put to right
Past misdeeds forgiven
If evil ebbed away in the flow of time and all
Vanished that was forbidden
Poverty and famine were forgotten and lost
All prospered and were glad
And if the cruelness of time and passing
Were to cease and let us stay
In the time so carefree and simple
When every time was a sunny day
All evil ebbed away in the flow
Of a magical miracle word
But, would all be swell and easy,
Was there one word to change the world?

Ellie Beech (12)
Etone College, Nuneaton

I Had A Dream

I had a dream, a song to sing,
I could not fly, I had no wings,
But the sky was grey,
It gave me a fright.
Mr Annoying was lingering about,
He made me want to scream and shout!

Josie Cross (13)
Etone College, Nuneaton

My Grandad

I wake up every morning
Thinking of my grandad,
How funny and unforgetful he is,
And all the good things
He has done for me.

My grandad, that always loves me,
Always there,
Just to care,
Whatever I do, wrong or right.

He takes me out to places
He gives me loads of money,
He is supportive and kind
And he always cheers my day up
With his loving, great big smile.

When night-time comes
And the moon and stars are shining brightly
In the dark, black sky.
My grandad comes and says goodnight
And I have a dream
That lasts all of the night,
That dream is about my grandad,
Always loyal and kind.

Maggie Barrow (12)
Etone College, Nuneaton

34

My Love Dream

The dream I always have is about
                                You.

My love
My dream
When I dream of you I want it to come
True
                        I want to be
                        With you.

My love
My dream
Your legs must be tired as you run through
                        My mind too
                        Much

My love
My dream
To the world you are one person to
                Me, you are the world

                My love
                My dream

        X I want to be with X
            X You X

Declan Goring (12)
Etone College, Nuneaton

Don't Do Drugs

Don't do drugs!
Don't become down and depressed if you don't feed your addiction,

Don't do drugs!
Do drugs and your family will disown you,

Don't do drugs!
Or you will become dirty and unhygienic,

Don't do drugs!
You will become aggressive to your family and friends,

Don't do drugs!
You will blow all your money and could become homeless,

Don't do drugs!
You could become a sly thief and steal from family and friends,

Don't do drugs!
Nobody wants to know a druggie!

Don't do drugs!
You could die of an overdose!

Time's ticking . . .
Get yourself clean and safe!

Don't do drugs!

Caine Hughes (11)
Etone College, Nuneaton

My Dream

I have a dream
To make a light beam
A light to the future
To see what I will be
To see what I can do
What this life brings to me
So let my dreams run free.

Daniel Simmons (12)
Etone College, Nuneaton

Belief

The angels and demons,
Pushing us on,
And holding us back,
Drowned by the eternal tears,
That will forever flow,
Stuck in the prison of hate, anger and pure nothing,
Always told you would be stuck in the same routine,
Like a cracked record,
Spiralling round and round,
While your life spirals down and down,
Global economy constantly oppressing
The glory that was once a life,
Now as the seeds of thought plant,
To make new blooming life,
Will the new adventure be different?
All anyone needs is a glimmer,
A spark,
A light at the end of your lashes,
To become a new blooming flower,
To do the stuff of your dreams,
All it takes
Is belief.

Matthew Riley (12)
Etone College, Nuneaton

My Mother

M y mother is always there for me.
O ther times when I am upset she still makes me feel happy.
T he times when she supports me, she makes me
    feel unbeatable.
H er words are so powerful, calm, as soft as a breeze.
E very day she cares for me and makes me stronger.
R arely does she argue with me.

Salman Lohiya (12)
Etone College, Nuneaton

Freedom

It crawls underneath our skin,
Hiding in the corners of our eyes,
We can feel it inside us,
Injustice.

What have we done to deserve this?
Treated like dirt,
Like we don't matter,
Like it's a crime to live.

Do our families know where we are?
That we are in this awful place?
I hope they don't,
Else our lives will be a disgrace.

But we will survive,
And we will live on,
And bells will ring,
A happy song.

A place full of light,
Where we are free,
And justice
Will find me.

Jenna Harris (11)
Etone College, Nuneaton

Untitled

The candle fades out
In the darkness,
Smoke forms little soldiers
In the dark sky.
The soldiers disappear,
They turn to people shaking hands,
Their world is happy,
But is ours?

Liam Bruntlett (12)
Etone College, Nuneaton

Candyland

Last night I had a dream about a
Place called Candyland,
It was cosy, warm and nice,
I was welcomed by a marching band.

Fountains of chocolate, pebbles of rock,
Toffee in piles, block by block.
Lemonade rivers and marshmallow dogs,
And hippety, hoppety gummy sweet frogs.

Sugar paper grass, clouds of candyfloss,
Fudge-covered lampposts and gelatine gloss.
Cake houses with Smarties for decoration,
What a wonderful sensation.

Then I wake up in the morning,
Thinking about my dream,
I know that it is not real,
Or so it may seem.

Last night I had a dream about a
Place called Candyland,
It was cosy, warm and nice,
I was seen out by a marching band.

Bethany Adler-Smith (12)
Etone College, Nuneaton

Knockout Dream

I have a dream to be in that ring,
Count to 10 and have a knockout,
Bang bang, straight down,
Blood everywhere;
In the corner rope, drowsy and dizzy,
He's lying down on the hospital bed.
Holding the golden belt up in the air,
The crowds screaming 'Yeah! Yeah! Yeah!'

Harry Wells (11)
Etone College, Nuneaton

No To War,
Yes To Love And Care

I say no to war
All the suffering and pain
What is the point?
There is no point.

We should be happy
With what we have
Not fighting for land
Life we should cherish, not land.

Imagine the world full of peace
People allowed to live their life
No hurt, no pain caused by war
No destruction anymore.

Just think of no clouds in the sky
The world is calm, cool and nice
The love and care we have
So what is the reason to fight?

I say no to war
But yes to love and care.

Cara Woodruff (11)
Etone College, Nuneaton

I Dream

I dream
Of you
Of me
How it was meant to be
For now
Forever
We are meant to be
Together.

Chloe Ekin (12)
Etone College, Nuneaton

40

Love For Boys

I give love for a few boys at my school,
They are the cutest boys I've ever seen,
They make me so happy on a very sad day,
I do love them.

When they are near I feel so happy,
They make me laugh when they tell jokes,
I feel safe and happy when I am at school
Because they are there,
I do love them.

Love is true from the heart,
But they don't know that I love them,
It is a special thing to have,
Love is a beautiful thing,
I do love them.

Love is true, love is really,
Love is what I truly feel,
I love them deep from my heart,
I will never let them go for
I love them
All.

Jennifer Gandy (12)
Etone College, Nuneaton

I Have A Dream

Sky and sun are blue and bright,
Nobody knows the meaning of fright.
Seas are clear, pollution faded away,
And people are happy, each and every day.
Wars have ended, gunfire ceased,
And all that's left is safety and peace.
Joy and happiness is all you feel
But dreams aren't always . . . real . . .

Matthew Leake (12)
Etone College, Nuneaton

Children Have Rights Too!

Physical fists flying
Across the sky,
Threats and forces,
I want to die.
Bruises and cuts,
Scars and pain,
Why do I have to suffer
In vain
When I could get hit
With a train?
If I can't gain help,
Will they gain power?
I think I'm gonna . . .
Die in the shower,
Pushes and pulls
As I tremble in fear,
How can it stop?
The answer is clear,
I need to . . .
Tell someone . . .
Very dear!

Alex Gill (12)
Etone College, Nuneaton

I Have A Dream

To do the best I can,
To touch the sky
And never wake up from this wonderful dream
Because the dream is all I have
And all I can hope is that
I will never wake up from this dream,
Because if I do I'll never dream of this . . .
Ever again.

Aliyah Bhikha (12)
Etone College, Nuneaton

My Two Grans

My two grans
This is for you
For all the pain you've been through.
My two grans
This is for you
Stronger together, than ever.
My two grans
Who never break out and cry
Even through all the pain
You both just smile like nothing's wrong.
My two grans
This is for you
You never show your pain
Even through all the hardship
You just smile like the shining moon.
My two grans
This is for you
Cancer can kill
But you came out golden.
My two grans
This is for you.

Saalihah Bilimoria (12)
Etone College, Nuneaton

Is This Really A Dream?

I have a dream about
Darkness and disaster
Everyone driving at 80 miles faster
Killing and death every night
Blood, gore and stabbing every fight.

Sunshine sets to grizzles ash-grey
Wondering if anyone would move this corpse
Out of my driveway.

Running through the street
Only watching our dreams get beat
As it falls on hard concrete
And seeing it all repeat.

Next day, a death on a railway
I guess, just an unfortunate
Event of misplay.

Looking up into the dreaded skyline
Thinking about how long it is
That is . . .
                 My lifeline.

Faizah Khalifa (14)
Etone College, Nuneaton

I Have A Dream

I have a dream
One day the world will seem
Relaxed and calm
And the world will inflict no harm
Day and night
There's guaranteed a fight
Put a stop to war
There should be more law
To love each other like they're your brother.

Hope Dunne (13)
Etone College, Nuneaton

This Is My Dream . . .

A world of death and destruction,
Of hate and assassins.
Or a world of life and beauty,
Of love and friendship and grins.

A grey colourless place,
Of building blocks and poison
And a place of red and green and blue
And a wide open horizon.

People who die too fast to count,
And happiness slowly washed away by the never-ending sea.
Or maybe a wonderful feeling,
That will always be free.

I chose the happy place,
The best place for me.
But life chose the broken world,
The worst place to be.

A sleeping dream . . .
A living nightmare . . .
What is *your* dream?

Eve Andrew (12)
Etone College, Nuneaton

Chocolate, Oh Chocolate

It I don't have fear I get desolate,
I sleep soundly and quiet with you by my side.
I would never leave you alone,
By your side I hide.
You shine in the light,
Nice and soft in your wrapper so light,
If I might
I will eat you,
My beautiful.

Ben Deacon (13)
Etone College, Nuneaton

Listen to Me!

Listen to me,
I am a victim, too scared to go to school.

Listen to me,
Nobody on my side, so I feel alone.

Listen to me,
No escape from the cyber-bullying. Happy slapping is so sad.

Listen to me,
Anger builds up as their insults are *negative. Negative,*
Nasty messages on MSN,
Worry builds up so I can't concentrate.

Listen to me,
I am afraid, frightened and scared,
Drip, drip, drip, as the tears drop.

Listen to me,
I am hungry because they took my lunch money.

Listen to me,
Their physical punches put me in hospital,
Stop bullying now and *listen to me!*

Thomas Slater (11)
Etone College, Nuneaton

The Dream

I have a dream
To change the world
To see beautiful boys and beautiful girls
To see people's happiness uncurl
Not to phone 999 just to know
Everything's fine.
Don't hide and stay away
Because one day the bad
It will go away.
Just stay
Get your pay
Don't go the bad way
Just to hear us speak
Never see our knees
Go weak.
Don't let them back you down with fear
Don't let them take a tear
Be brave my dear
Because everyone cares for you.

And that's my dream.

Thomas Smith (12)
Etone College, Nuneaton

Fairy Tales

Once upon a time
In a world of make-believe
When we were all children
Patient and naive,
The world was a magic place
Filled with sunlit sky,
We liked to just sit there
And let the real world pass us by.
Princesses stared down at us
From their stony towers
And ordinary objects
Beheld extraordinary powers.

Living in a fairytale,
Too childish to see
That everything we thought we knew
Was simply just a dream.

Ten years on and the magic has all but gone,
A world of grey with the sparkle washed away.

Kim Neale (13)
Etone College, Nuneaton

We Want . . .

We want peace not war,
We want all people to be equal,
We want bullying to break free,
We want arsonists
To realise what trouble they are causing for us,
We want child abuse to come to a stop
And those poor children to find a voice,
We want people to stop smoking
And putting their lives at risk,
We want to change . . .

Ellis Nicole-Webb (12)
Etone College, Nuneaton

48

The Three

The three, the three
That changed me,
The three, the three
That helped me,
The three, the three
That cared for me,
The three, the three,
They inspired me!

The old, the grey was one,
The tall, the fun was two,
The kind, the caring was three,
And you know me!

A poem for you and for me
Mr Vickers,
Mr Pybus,
Mrs Delbridge,
And me.

Lucy Parlett (12)
Etone College, Nuneaton

I Have A Dream . . .

It was a magical place
Knitted with gold lace
A mysterious face appeared,
'This world is evil,' then he disappeared,
The gold lace twisted and turned
And a raging fire burned.

The place I thought was Heaven is Hell
And there was no one to tell
I began to burn
My stomach began to churn
Then I awoke . . .

Jamie Bull (12)
Etone College, Nuneaton

49

Save My World

Sitting in a dark, dingy corner
Skin and bone placed upon my legs
Rags laid on my skin to get warmer
Not knowing of a warm cushioned bed,

Miles and miles of parched barren sand
Mouth dry as a desert
Eyes full of hard gritty sand
No comfort and hope within us,

Illness and poverty linger around
Boxes and boxes of death on a stand
Betrayed as an anchor pulling me to the ground
Can anybody hear our calling?

Money and hope would do our world some good
Belief to grow our land
To rid away of death and blood
My life can be saved and lived as it should.

Chloe Worth (12)
Etone College, Nuneaton

I Have A Dream

I have a dream
To win the league
For Nuneaton's football team
And score the winning goal
In the league
For the team
And the atmosphere is all.

I have a dream
To be the captain
For the team
And lift them up the leagues
For my loyal team.

Kyle Brandon (12)
Etone College, Nuneaton

An Inspiring Hero

I have been inspired by Steven Segal
Who tries not to yell.
He stands up for himself
With his pockets full with wealth.

Devastation has been brought to the world
With a gun melted and curled.
Bullets have been shot
Making holes in a yacht.

There was a baby in a cot,
Through the devastation got shot.
Fires and riots have been made
By people from the Mafia who get paid.

You've got to be brave,
'Cause you cannot be pushed around like a slave,
Make a stand for yourself,
And you'll remain in good health.

Junaid Khan (12)
Etone College, Nuneaton

I Have A Dream

When I grow up
I dream of me
Playing for a football team
Scoring a goal
Then I will know
I can win the football league.

Be a millionaire
Buy a Lamborghini
And travel the world
And see all I can see
Come back
Then I have lived my dream.

Rory Betteridge (12)
Etone College, Nuneaton

We Shouldn't Destroy The World

The world is full of war and destruction,
The reason to fight is less and less,
The last generation fought for us,
So we shouldn't destroy the world.

We should realise how lucky we are,
We have clean water, food, shelter,
We are more fortunate than most,
So we shouldn't destroy the world.

We have all we need, but what do we want?
Land, money, power?
Why should we need it, we are fine as we are;
So we shouldn't destroy the world.

All of this, it is true,
No more people black and blue,
We should leave the world as it is,
And we shouldn't destroy the world.

Sophie Evans (11)
Etone College, Nuneaton

Smoking

Smoking is wrong
It makes your head go wrong
It could make you die
You will start to lie
You could get cancer
Then you cannot become a dancer
You will think it's cool
But you're breaking the rules.
Why be a chancer
Because you will get cancer?
It will give you disease
Your family won't be pleased!

Matthew Longbottom (12)
Etone College, Nuneaton

I Have A Dream

I have a dream
That one day there would be no violence or upset,
I don't know when that day will come,
I hope it will be sometime after sunset.

I'd love to see love and happiness,
But all I see is hatred and unhappiness
I'd love to stop this,
But I don't think I can,
Without a helping hand.

And now I've got my friends to help,
And they think it's a great idea,
And now we're ready to go and stop this awful madness,
But I've just woke up and found it was just a dream.

But now I've found out,
The world is full of love and happiness,
And I am as happy as can be.

Jordan Aubrey (12)
Etone College, Nuneaton

I Have A Dream

I have a dream to be the
Best I want to be,
I have a dream that will always be a dream,
I dream of you,
I dream of me,
I have a dream which will remain a dream,
A dream can ever come true,
A dream will be true,
Everyone can have a dream,
I dream of you crying,
I dream of you laughing,
This relationship will be true.

Jaskiran Kang (12)
Etone College, Nuneaton

53

Dream

Every night I have a dream,
A dream to flow along a stream,
Stars in Heaven, oh so bright,
As they shimmer through the night.

Fields so green and oceans so wide,
Beauty that is extremely hard to hide,
As you fall down spiral stairs,
You see your worries, pasts and cares.

As you dream, the puppeteer cries,
As your dream . . . fades and dies,
When you're awake you're really alone,
As you remorse on decaying bone.

As you cry on ivy stone
Slowly your heart begins to moan,
It fills with sadness, hatred and devastation,
As it suddenly burst in deflation.

Macaulay Hancox (12)
Etone College, Nuneaton

Children Need A Life Too!

It was horrible, more than horrible,
Why were they doing this to me?
I witnessed everything that happened to me,
As I saw violence throughout my eyes,
It's no surprise
That my temper started to rise,
I needed help that was plain to see,
All of the voices going inside of me,
I started to whisper,
But then I roared,
Overjoyed the burden had gone,
Now I can do what I want.

Melissa Burgess (12)
Etone College, Nuneaton

The Smoke Of Ignorance

As the crimson rain never stops,
Eyes of lust, fear and determination widen.
The ground-shaking-growing-mounded with men,
They sorrowfully call for you.
Spirits proudly climb up, in memory of loved ones.
Grey and purple sky, darkening,
As wisps of smoke pirouette up and down repetitively.
The stars sing in harmony with the moon,
Before the barrier of smoke, a serenity,
A peaceful sanctuary.
Behind the barrier - imaginary.
If reality transformed to fiction
Would life be perfect and tranquil?
Or would the world be bare and numb?
Vanity and pride leads to destruction,
A touch of hope,
A glimpse of freedom.

Hope Newton (11)
Etone College, Nuneaton

Many A Man

Many a man follows his dream;
Whether it to go far into space,
Or be part of the winning team.
I have a dream to be living at a steady pace.
Maybe I could save the world,
Help stop the wars all over the place.
And wouldn't it be grand
To find the lost city of the underworld.
If I had the power to put the past away
I would lock it tightly, far, far away.

Ella Albrighton (12)
Etone College, Nuneaton

Dreams

Dreams inspire us,
They fill our minds
With luxurious specialties,
We live in hope
For a chance
To turn them into reality.

We each have a different dream
For who we are,
Whether you're loud or quiet,
Big or small,
We each have dreams
That live in us all.

They fill us up with happiness
As our hearts get broken,
We live to fulfil our destiny
For however long it may be.

Hannah Rice (11)
Etone College, Nuneaton

My Dream

I have a dream
To fly up high
And soar my soul
In the twilight!

I have a dream
To touch the moon
Grab a star
And dance on Neptune.

My dreams are big
Random and bright
But that makes me
Feel alright!

Charlotte Quinn (12)
Etone College, Nuneaton

Racism, Walk Away

Angry racists scar your mind
Their words are cruel, leave them
Behind.
Don't worry, ignore them
For each day the hateful words they say
Turns the blue into concrete-grey.

We have to have hope
To cope
With the misery
With a smile
And know that we are better
For we are true
For we are free
To write, to fight
To offer light and the right
To a better life.

Adeel Rashid (12)
Etone College, Nuneaton

We Have A Wish

We have a wish,
A wish
That there's no wars,
Just peace.
There's no pain,
Just happiness.
We wish people were equal,
No boys better than girls . . .
Just the same.
We wish people didn't take drugs,
Just nice clean people.
We wish people weren't homeless,
Just a nice great home.

Brandon Northall (12)
Etone College, Nuneaton

To Make The World

I have a dream
To make the world a place
To be united as one,
To live in a world
Where everyone knows your name.

I have a dream to make
The world an eco-friendly place,
Where every race
Will be joined together.

I have a dream that
All animals will roam freely,
And a place where no one likes to steal.

I have a dream to make
The world a place
Where we will be united as one.

Jordan Bloomer (14)
Etone College, Nuneaton

War Never Changes

Bombs drop,
Lives are lost,
A barren wasteland is created,
The scattered remains of a once great society,
Bones perish under the inhospitable wasteland floor,
The streets ablaze,
The world suffers under the strain of nuclear warfare,
Countries crumble,
Continents wiped off the map,
Everything dies,
Death and destruction follow anything in its path,
This is our future,
But only if we choose it.

Nicholas Watmough (11)
Etone College, Nuneaton

Poverty

One child sits alone, thirsty, starving,
'Why can't there be food?' she moans,
'This isn't very charming.'

Every day she's by herself, wandering the streets,
But nobody cares,
She doesn't have the strength any more,
But still nobody cares.

What if poverty vanished,
All of the children wouldn't be famished,
Imagine the happiness, imagine the smiles,
What wouldn't they give for a life like ours?

Weaker and weaker she grows,
But what she doesn't know,
Is we have the money to fix it,
Just to save a life, it only costs a little bit.

Jessica Owen (11)
Etone College, Nuneaton

Bullying

The memories will never fade,
The pain will always be there,
I will forgive but never forget,
On the days I felt unwanted,

Those days haunt me day by day,
As I look in thin air It's always happening,
Lunchtimes I felt lonely
On the days I felt unwanted,

Thinking I was nothing,
Thinking I was stupid,
These thoughts will never go,
On the days I felt unwanted.

Ayesha Pathan (12)
Etone College, Nuneaton

My Dream

Just imagine a world
With no peas
Carrots or broccoli for lunch.

No one telling me
To tidy up my room

No getting up for school

No lights out by 10

Endless supply of sweets

Watching TV when I want

Playing with friends
Instead of homework

Not a care in the world
That's my dream.

Megan French (12)
Etone College, Nuneaton

I Have A Dream

Being my own person,
That's what I believe;
Following my own dreams,
That's what I'll achieve.

I won't blend in with the crowd,
I'll say what I think;
Anger and uproar,
They're coming to the brink.

The truth must be told,
Life isn't all strawberries and cream;
I am my own person,
I will follow my dream.

Melissa Burrows (12)
Etone College, Nuneaton

60

I Wish

I wish
That all drugs had never been discovered,

I wish
That all riots had never been started,

I wish
All child abuse had never happened,

I wish
Bullying never existed,

I wish
All arsonists never did what they do,

I wish
The Yorkshire Ripper was never born,

I wish . . . I wish . . . I wish . . .

Cory Richardson (12)
Etone College, Nuneaton

Angels

I dream of angels

Their graceful wings
At a graceful pace
As they smile at me
With their innocent face

Their flowing white robes
Their curly hair
Their glowing halos
That they wear with flair

I start floating
High in the sky
I see a bright light
And realise I have died!

Georgina Burdon-Gibbons (12)
Etone College, Nuneaton

Mum

She's my world, my life, my everything,
Trying to make changes for the better,
She tackles every obstacle in life.
She supports and helps me,
Life is too short to fall out with her,
We'll never know what tomorrow will bring,
But we'll stick together till the very end.
What will happen if I lose her?
I'll be abandoned without happiness,
Abandoned without love.

No one can ever be like my mum,
No one can ever replace her,
It's not all the time you get a mum like mine,
Especially when she's got that strong everlasting love.
She's my world, my life, my everything . . .

Mariam Mahmood (12)
Etone College, Nuneaton

I Have A Dream

My name is Bruno, no, no, no
It is cool being tall
I get to swim in my pool
I want to play for my football team
Because I rule.
I will live in a small town of Assisi
It is cool
I live in a house bigger than my mouse
With flat-screen TVs all over the house
My Ferrari is my dream car
I ride around it like a star
I've passed my exams so hear me out
My name is Bruno
And I am going out.

Bruno Brunozzi-Jones (12)
Etone College, Nuneaton

I Have A Dream!

The sun is setting in the evening sky
The wind blowing in my hair
The birds are singing their final chorus

The laughs and giggles of children slowly fade away
Soon I am left alone on a beach of golden sand
Staring out at the shining blue sea

As night falls, silver stars start to appear in the dark blue sky
I sit down and breathe in the fresh salty air
Smiling about how good it feels

I stand up
Shake off all the sand
Which falls to the ground
Like fairy dust
And walk off into the night sky . . .

Chelsea Palmer (12)
Etone College, Nuneaton

My Worst Nightmare

My worst nightmare
Is a world without a care,
A place of blood and guts
From explosions to cuts.

Knives, a gun
And a blocked-out sun.
Someday I'll have some real dreams
Where the sun shines and the sea gleams.

I hope I wake up soon
In the light of the silver moon
To keep me in the comfort of my lair,
And tear me from this nightmare.

Levi Cave (12)
Etone College, Nuneaton

63

Free

I'm tired of being what you want me to be,
Like you are the leader of my life,
So I've started rebelling to be like me.
Put under the pressure of walking in your shoes,
I don't want to follow you.
I wanna be free, I wanna be able to choose.
Every step that I take is another mistake to you,
I couldn't care less, I wanna find out on my own.
I don't even know who I am anymore or my friend's foe.
I've become so numb, I can't feel you there.
I can't think for myself anymore, you are my senses.
You are like my eyes, giving everybody a dirty stare.
All I want to do is be more like me and be less like you,
But I have come to my senses and I'm determined,
I will be me and I will see this through.

Alex Davies (12)
Etone College, Nuneaton

No School!

I always have a dream,
Where I'm in front of a TV screen.
There's never any school,
Just chilling in a swimming pool,
I don't do any work,
Just drive round in a Merc,
I can do what I like,
I can go for a hike,
So I wish there was no school,
'Cause then I can rule!

Muhammad Patel (12)
Etone College, Nuneaton

A World Without . . .

A world without vandals
A world without abuse
A world without war
That's not going to happen,
It'll never work
We'll all die from a bullet of lead.
A world in our head
We have water and bread,
But in the real world we aren't at all fed.
Most people say war is all gore
But people who say that are awfully wrong,
War is racism, discrimination and bullying.
We don't need guns,
All we need is a wise man's words
To stop a war, bullies and vandals.

Ben Simoniti (12)
Etone College, Nuneaton

I Have A Dream

Football is my dream.
When I grow up I want to play for the Man U team,
I want to lift the Cups
And live my dreams.
I want to win the captain's band
And live near the sea and the sand.
My dream is to play for my national team
And win the cups of my dream
When I win all of my money
I will buy a Lamborghini or maybe a Ferrari.

Corey Hopewell (12)
Etone College, Nuneaton

Dreams And Nightmares

Dreams are nightmares,
Nightmares are dreams,
They all are the same,
Or so it seems!

Dreams are flowers, fields and sunsets,
Nightmares are dragons, monsters and upsets.
I don't care which one I'm in,
As long as they have gone and been.
Dreams hold your future life,
Nightmares hold your future wife!

Dreams are nightmares,
Nightmares are dreams.
They all are the same,
Or so it seems!

Alister Davis (12)
Etone College, Nuneaton

War And Racism

What's wrong with black and white?
We're all a family, stood in the light,
Words of hatred ring through ears,
This should now stop after all these years.
To walk in the street light, full of fear,
I sense that something bad is near.

Guns, bombs and children crying,
These are the things that leave people lying,
Bullets flying and leaving dead,
War should not happen, so the Lord said.
Terrorists linger and wait to blow,
Looking for those buildings lined in a row.

But time ago I heard God say,
'Keep the hope and it will stop some day.'

Liam Hutchinson (12)
Etone College, Nuneaton

The Dream

Every poem has a theme,
This one's about a man who dreamed,
About a world with children black and white
Who would play and not fight.
He wanted peace for all the world,
He always told people to never give up.
Every black person was treated unfair,
But he done that powerful dare.
That man's name was Martin Luther King,
And that's how he changed everything.

Terry Thiedeman (12)
Etone College, Nuneaton

My Wish . . .

Bullying is really bad,
Say you were a clever boy,
And you really liked school,
Then a 'bully' came over and started bullying you,
And they did this every single day,
That would ruin your life!

If you're bad you're bad,
If you're good you're good,
But just remember not to be a bully . . .

Josh Harrison (11)
Etone College, Nuneaton

I Have A Dream

I have a dream; that one day on the Earth,
the people of Iraq will sit with Americans
at the table of brotherhood.
As God said they should.

I have a dream; that one day everyone will be loved.
This is my hope and faith.
With this faith we will be able to be peaceful forever.

I have a dream; involving a peaceful, harmonious brook.
Not polluted by the besmirching it has took.

I have a dream; of an unpublicised world,
where private is personal and gossip isn't swirled.

I have a dream; that Kate Shepard was an idol, not an example,
with achievements far from ample.

I have a dream; that explorers were naturalists and man-made,
not historians on parade.

I have a dream; that the world was rid of murderers, arsonists and criminals
and full of environmentalists, vetinarians and intellectuals.

I have a dream; of a lifetime wihout worry and regret,
carelessness and upset.

I have a dream; that it was the end of the global finance contingency,
The end of all stringency.

I have a dream; that there is no such thing as carbon emissions and global
warming.
No Gordon Brown, misinforming.

I have a dream; that foreign aid be prominent,
No more US government rules to be dominant.

I have a dream; that the Universal Declaration of Human Rights
will actually come into play,
no more disarray.

I have a dream; that Americans never said, 'They sold you slaves, when
they themselves couldn't even work on Labour Day.'
It isn't that they're black or white, their hands are in areas shades of grey.

I have a dream; that I'm not judged by where I'm from, who I know, what I

have, whether or not I'm in poverty.
That values are important, so prioritising uncontrollably.

I have a dream; that there were no cakes sent into jail with a saw blade in
them to help jail break,
But there is harmony between man . . . for heaven's sake.

I have a dream; I had a best friend who was hard as stone with hidden fears
She loved in a silence that no one hears.

I have a dream; American fires would hindrance
Give residents a fighting chance.

I have a dream; that vulnerable children are protected
Less social cases being neglected.

I have a dream; people took a stand on child poverty
and no one suffered.

I have a dream; UK banks were safe from insolvency,
Less endangered by abundancy.

I have a dream; there was no such word as 'terrorism',
But paths free of antagonism.

I have a dream; that sport is a leisure,
Not all all-round displeasure.

I have a dream
I would have believed all the dreams. In realms of despair,
If it wasn't for rude awakenings and a reality scare.
Yet to dream and I'd discover what could have been,
If I'd only closed my eyes a bit longer, I might have another dream
One of happiness and radiance.

Shannon Purcell (14)
Madeley High School, Crewe

Inspirational

I can move a mountain,
I can stop a war,
I can solve the money crisis with one hand,
I can create worlds,
I can fly a plane; I can drive a jet boat,
I can build a river,
I can save the rainforest with one eye blindfolded.

But who do I admire?
How do I aspire?
When will I achieve these things?
Why am I running in rings?
What am I trying to do?
Where was I when I looked up at *you*?

I can sharpen a pencil,
I can feel the Earth,
I can keep a fish (just about alive),
I can wash my hands,
I can nurture and maintain a garden,
I can cook a meal,
I can achieve anything I want to do!

But who do I admire?
How do I aspire?
My mum, dad, brother, fish?
Maybe the fruit dish?
Mrs Tetley, Ms Pattinson, Mrs Griffies (she made me) or Tom?
Dance, music, TV or a CD Rom?

I can hear,
I can eat,
I can see,
I can drink,
I can taste,
I can smell.
I can feel.

But who do I admire?
How do I aspire?
Everyone, anyone, you!

How about what I left in the loo?
Barrack Obama, Simon Cowell
Or maybe my constant scowl?

I thank you for listening to me,
I bet you're as bored as me,
Pray let me win,
Because I'm warning you, I have a pin!
Thank you for inspiring me,
Now I really need a . . .

Oliver Jones (12)
Madeley High School, Crewe

Famine

This world we live in; fair or not?
Poverty here and there,
Third World countries in huge fear,
For death's now everywhere.

The children; poor, thin and frail,
Hoping for some aid,
Let's pray that light will shine on them;
A harmony to be made.

The suffering, the helplessness,
Who knows what they're to do?
For all they wish for, night on night;
A pot of home-made stew!

One cannot imagine,
The pain young ones go through,
The fear they may never live,
A life they could pursue.

But
A channel of hope runs through the town,
When Oxfam come to stay,
Spend the money, spend the time;
Give another day.

Claire Hemingway (13)
Madeley High School, Crewe

Introvert

I'm not easy going,
I am complicated,
I don't like to think later,
I like to think first,
I'm not emotional,
I am relaxed.

I am who I am.

I don't want action,
I want ideas,
I don't want noise or variety,
I want quiet and concentration,
I don't want a lot of people,
I want one-on-one.

I am who I am.

I don't want to go fast,
I like my life to be slow,
I don't want to rush,
I like to be patient,
I don't want to be interrupted,
I like to finish the job.

I am who I am.

I don't want to be loud,
I want to be private,
I don't like to remember things,
I want to write down my memories,
I'm not outgoing,
I want to be calm.

I am who I am.

I don't want to be interpersonal,
I want to be intrapersonal,
I don't like to start a conversation,
I prefer to join a conversation,

I don't want to change the world,
I want to understand the world.

I am who I am.
And what I am is my own man.

Aaron Hodges (13)
Madeley High School, Crewe

I Have A Dream

I have a dream,
A dream to live,
To live until I am a hundred.

I have a dream,
A dream to win,
To win the lottery.

I have a dream,
A dream to have children,
A dream to see them grow up and raise their own children.
For them to be a lawyer, a doctor or a teacher
The best job they deserve
And I will be the proudest mum there will ever be.

I have a dream,
A dream to have,
To have a three day weekend.

I have a dream,
A dream to have,
The best job in the world,
A teacher, a lawyer or a candlestick maker.

I have a dream,
A dream for people
To be as happy as possible.

I have a dream,
A dream to live
The best possible life I can lead!

Natalie Sutcliffe (14)
Madeley High School, Crewe

Invisible Children

A few countries south
A few countries west
On the continent of Africa
In the country of Uganda

A man called Joe Kony
Pretends to know spirits
Tries to be in charge but gets . . . rejected.

His pretend knowledge of spirits
Has gained him some followers,
They go into homes
And abduct the children.

These kids are forced
Into a life of misery
Taken before Kony
Whose hair is in braids.

They fear him at once
Follow his commands
Are issued with guns
And orders to kill.

If they protest or even sob
The punishment is harsh,
Death to siblings
Or mutilation to themselves.

Why is Kony still there?
Why won't he sign a peace document?
Some kids know no life
Other than the misery.

Invisible children
An organisation to help these kids,
Needs your help;
Stop the horrors.

It has spread - Sudan or Ethiopia
Why the misery?
Where have we been,
These last 23 years?

Help these kids,
Help invisible children,
Save them from
Kony and misery.

Marianne Drijfhout (12)
Madeley High School, Crewe

Mums

Our mums are unique to us,
Our mums are special,
After all - they gave birth to us,
So we owe them a lot.

I'm pretty glad I've got my mum,
She's persevered through her life,
She's not let anyone mess her around,
Mum's really important in my life.

Our mums work quite hard,
To nurture us to adulthood,
Constantly on the brink of loving to pestering
But you've got to admire them even so.

When my mum is afraid,
She tries hard not to show it
Because she does her best to be brave.
She even uses her little phrase, 'Head butt the problem,'
It's actually quite helpful.

Our mums are upset
As they see us leave home
But in the end they know
They've done their best and feel proud.

I'm happy I've got my mum,
She's wonderful in my opinion
But of course we'll find our own mums super
Because they really are.

Helena Gordon (12)
Madeley High School, Crewe

Walt Disney

Mickey Mouse came in 1928
when Walt Disney was travelling
with his soulmate.
He first thought of Brer Rabbit,
he thought he was great,
until Mickey Mouse came and filled the whole plate.
He drew different cartoons,
which came to life,
in his house,
it's Mickey Mouse.
He thought of ideas and came up with a plan,
to build a land called Disneyland.
where his characters had fun all day
I wish I was like him in every way.
creative and inspirational,
he meant a lot to the world
sharing ideas with his friends.
with the paintbrush brushing this way and that,
Mickey Mouse will never end.
Mickey Mouse is the good one,
when evil comes along,
the only way to get rid of it
is to sing a happy song.
Dreams came true
everywhere he went
in the Magic Kingdom
his life well spent.
This is the end for Walt Disney's first dream
but there is more to come, wait and see
because,
everywhere Walt Disney is there.

Amy Evans (13)
Madeley High School, Crewe

Stoke City

At the Britannia Stadium,
The cauldron of noise
Play Stoke City
Pulis and the boys.

The players come out the tunnel,
Hull and the red and whites,
Ready for another game,
Vital in the top flight.

'Why, why, why Delilah?'
The fans sing in delight,
As Fuller scores the opening goal,
Never giving up without a fight.

Fifteen minutes to go,
Lawrence takes a shot,
Looking for those three points,
Stoke have taken the lot.

And the roof comes off,
The away fans over the moon,
Lawrence scores from 25 yards
Survival is coming very soon.

The referee blows his whistle,
2-1 to Stoke the fans sing,
Pulis cheers to his supporters
Another season will soon be ending.

The three points are ours,
The Potters are finally safe,
Time for the champagne to be opened,
Survival, we can now celebrate.

Joe Smith (13)
Madeley High School, Crewe

A Poem For Who Inspires Me

Ms Pattinson inspires me
Including Miss Griffiths
So I want to be a teacher
And tell the kids the features.

Ms Pattinson is . . .

P erfect, like a bird
A mazing like she is
T errific like a sweet fizz
T alented as on 'Britain's Got Talent'
I ntelligent as an owl
N ever-ending gossiper
S uper like a super star
O ver the top
N ice as a nice biscuit.

Miss Griffiths is . . .

G reat like a free bird
R emarkable
I ndependent
F abulous
F antastic like the Fantastic Four
I nspires me
T errific like a superhero
H ilarious like a laughing hyena
S uper like a superstar.

These two people have inspired me
Since I was in Year 7
Now I believe I can follow my dream.

Tara-Louise Jennings (12)
Madeley High School, Crewe

78

Tomorrow!

I have a dream that tomorrow,
The trees will be green,
The birds will sing,
The flowers will bloom,
The sheep will bleat.

I have a dream that tomorrow,
The wind will whistle,
The rain won't pour,
The sun will shine,
The snow won't melt.

I have a dream that tomorrow,
The phone will ring,
The kettle will boil,
The microwave will ding,
The washer will spin.

I have a dream that tomorrow,
The cars will rush by,
The planes will stay in the sky,
The trains will run,
The people will walk.

I will wake,
I will listen,
I will touch,
I will see,
I have a dream for tomorrow.

Sophie Challinor (13)
Madeley High School, Crewe

My Heart Or My Soul

Thumping, thumping faster and faster
It's like my master
What should I choose
My heart or my soul?

Lead me here or lead me there
Life is full of choices
What should I choose
My heart or my soul?

Panicking now
Help me
What should I choose
My heart or my soul?

It's an everlasting choice
It will never end
What should I choose
My heart or my soul?

This choice is important
It could change my life
What should I choose
My heart or my soul?

I will never choose
It will always be a demanding question
What should I choose
My heart of my soul?

Zara Lovatt (12)
Madeley High School, Crewe

80

My Inspiration

Writes stories, songs and poems,
Blonde hair and blue eyes,
Wears baggy trousers with Converse
And is famous for her ties.

Grew up with the lads,
Learnt life their way,
Skating and rocking out
Life was OK.

But she had a dream,
An inspiration she could feel,
Then when she turned 16,
The dream became real.

She has never looked back,
She has achieved what she has tried,
She says she is determined,
To sing until she dies.

She inspired me to play guitar,
To dream and try my best,
To never give up on what I want,
And not listen to the rest.

So my inspiration comes from this,
From a childhood dream,
A Canadian singer,
Avril Lavigne.

Sophie Hewitt (13)
Madeley High School, Crewe

Friends

I have a dream
an image to see
they were standing there
looking at me

They stood there smiling
right at me
that is when it started
our friendship forever

We stood right there
our hands to hands
we flew into the open
watching the days grow old

We ran round a tree
leaves falling on the ground
it must have been spring
the day that we met

The time had come
she had to go
snowfall on her
but I know she was there.

Today I can still remember
the friendship that we had
she was always there
crossing streams of wonder.

Bethany Lewis (13)
Madeley High School, Crewe

Anyone Can Be A Hero

When I have a dream
I dream where people can,
Ordinary people like you and me
Who have jobs and school like us
But our story is set in a nearby town
Where a robber is waiting in the oil-slick shadows
And an old lady knows there's danger around this corner
The leather handbag is pulled between them both
Straining its fibres to stay in one position
While someone watches in the crimson night
To help this poor old soul
He wears a mask to hide his features
And when he jumps and lands
He uses his right fist and left leg
And knocks the muggers out
Even though he is skinny
His bendy arm still shows the strength
The sparkle in his eye radiates his warm heart
He bends and collects the bag
And hands it to the exhausted lady
He stands and looks heroic
And his motto always goes
'Anyone can help and
anyone can become a hero'
and this is what happens in this world of mine.

Reuben Speed (14)
Madeley High School, Crewe

Hold It Close And Tight

Listen to a heartbeat, hold it close and tight
Always ponder deeply, long into the night.

Make your presence widely known
As every person should greatly be shown.

Keep your family close by you
As you will need them as they need you.

A present will be lovingly admired
So buy them something that is greatly desired.

Make their presence widely known
As every person should greatly be shown.

Keep these people close by you
As you will need them as they need you.

Your friends are the family you mostly trust
So keep them close by you, cos you simply must.

Listen to the person who gives you the advice
And always thank them deeply for being so precise.

Many men will come and see
That friends should stick together just like you and me.

Listen to your friends and hold them close and tight
And ponder with them deeply throughout all your life.

Chelsea Cartwright (14)
Madeley High School, Crewe

Police

Police are fearless and inspiring
They get low wages
High workload.
They are caring and helpful
A big inspiration
They stop crime and save lives.

Jonathan Breeze (13)
Madeley High School, Crewe

The Death Of The Dog - Continued

(In memory of Boe Sorrentino 01-04-09 - RIP)

Two friends, they look so sad,
This was the walk that was very, very bad.

We got to the hill,
I felt a chill,
This was the place of the nasty kill.

We collected flowers,
To show our respect,
We wanted to show him that he was the best.

We got to the spot,
The point where it happened,
We broke into tears,
And out came the fears.

We stood for a while,
Then we both gave a smile,
And off we went to walk the final mile.

Still to this day we haven't looked back,
We will never regret it,
And we will never forget him.

Imogen Handforth (13)
Madeley High School, Crewe

Fire, Firefighter

Every day you risk your life
Every day you save a life
Every day you have that weird look on your face
That says, 'I can't believe that happened!'
Every day you fight a fire monster and win
Every day you come home and you go to bed
But that's you, a firefighter,
And I wouldn't want it any other way.

Zak Bagguley (12)
Madeley High School, Crewe

Hope

Keep your dreams alive,
Never stop believing
For one day they should come true,
All that is needed is hope.

Together we shall make a stand,
And wave goodbye to violence,
Peace shall come - be patient!
For all that is needed is hope.

Imagine living in a world without pain,
Wouldn't that be great?
Pain may be undefeatable,
But all that is needed is hope.

A new beginning is all we need,
Or a fresh start shall do,
You are never far from the final steps,
All that is needed is hope.

Inspiration is all it takes,
A bit of imagination,
Fight for what you believe in,
All that is needed is . . . hope.

Hannah King (14)
Madeley High School, Crewe

The Sound Of A Drum

Without drums music would be dry,
Without drums music would make you sigh,
Without the sound of the snare, the cymbal,
Sound would be bare, boredom, nimble.
Pop, metal, rock, blues
Without the drums there would be no tunes.
I found an inspiration in all things loud,
To be a drummer and to be so proud.

Tom Baddeley (13)
Madeley High School, Crewe

Last Of The Summer Rides

I mounted up in the last of the sunlight
I started off slowly
Then a walk, then a trot, then a canter
Hoping a gallop just might.

The wind dashing through my hair
Horses whinnies through the air
Waiting for the jump I dare
Here we go.

Memories flooding back to me
How we used to ride together
Then he went and left me be
We used to do this with glee.

How I always waited for him
Every night without fail
Ever since my world has been grim
I miss our rides so much.

Then a snap back to reality
Another passing day
I dismounted
And led my horse away.

Ellie Beeston (13)
Madeley High School, Crewe

Barack Obama

Barack Obama stands on his own two feet
With courage and wisdom in all that he speaks
People are making a change no matter their background
Whether they're black or white or don't have a pound.
Many are standing up for what they believe
And for once people have hope in what they can achieve
He is the face of the people's dreams coming true
There is hope for the world in all that he'll do.

Nina Harris (13)
Madeley High School, Crewe

Ryan Shawcross

He's big, he's tall
He makes players fall
'It's Shawcross!'
'It's Shawcross!'

He wears red and white
He never loses a fight
'It's Shawcross!'
'It's Shawcross!'

He never gives up
If we lose the cup
'It's Shawcross!'
'It's Shawcross!'

When attackers come near
He gives them fear
'It's Shawcross!'
'It's Shawcross!'

When he plays the game
People cheer his name
'It's Shawcross!'
'It's Shawcross!'

Nathan Smith (13)
Madeley High School, Crewe

My Dad

My dad, where do I start?
The best by far.
Laughing, caring, all in one.
Someone I can always count on.
Making a dim candle into a sparkling flame.
Bringing a light of joy
Love and gain
I love you, Dad.

Jack Salt (13)
Madeley High School, Crewe

What Is Inspiration?

I'm sitting in the classroom,
The theme is inspiration,
I rack my brains but all I get,
Is a lot of perspiration.

The boy is inspired by a footballer,
The girl next to me writes about her mum,
Where do they get their ideas from?
I just wish I had some.

This task is driving me crazy,
I need more motivation,
It's not that I'm not trying,
I'm desperate for some stimulation.

I'm trying to think who inspires me,
The list is pitifully short,
I need to get a move on,
Before I get distraught.

The minute hand moves so slowly,
Time's almost finished, nearly done,
I look outside - there's the answer!
I'm inspired by *everyone!*

Sneha Alexander (14)
Madeley High School, Crewe

Football Fantasy

My dream would be to be a striker for Manchester United,
Running onto the pitch with the crowd roaring my name out.
I felt like a legend for 78,000 fans,
Like a sea of faces staring back at me.
At Old Trafford, that's where I want to be.
The smell of the turf beneath me,
Taking charge of the ball, feeling free.

Harry Salmon (14)
Madeley High School, Crewe

I Have A Dream

As I stand in the field,
Armies form a defensive shield.
Bullets rip through the ground,
Gunshot is the only sound.
Planes fly high in the sky,
Neither side can afford to be shy.

Bombs fall on either side,
Vehicles overturn and then collide.
Death is everywhere,
How can this be fair?

I have a dream,
In which no one is supreme.
Where all firearms are laid down,
And life can get on without a frown.
I have a dream,
And it starts here!

Speak your mind,
And we will find,
A way to end war,
Now!

Thomas Bladen-Hovell (13)
Madeley High School, Crewe

Fellaini's Afro

Fellaini's afro
It's the best it can be
I love his great hair
That's why he inspires me!

His hair cannot get any better
It's so curly and so big
That's why I am growing my hair
Instead of buying a wig!

Joe Morris (13)
Madeley High School, Crewe

War Poem

Let's show respect for those people who died,
Fighting to save our lives,
For we would not be here today without soldiers fighting;
Bombs, guns, fire crackers, it's all frightening.

Through the trenches, through the war,
To stop and walk away all they had to do was open that army tank door,
For they did not give up or walk away,
Stayed fighting until the dawn of day.

WWI, WWII were both dreadful times,
I suppose life is full of murder and crime,
Soldiers are the saviours of the day,
For all they have done for us, forget them? No way!
That's why we have 11th November, Remembrance Day.

For we do not know all the facts and figures,
Like how many people? Did they have diggers?
May their souls rest in peace,
That's all we can do at least.

For this is a dream for us, but cruelty for them
Bless their souls and may they rest in peace.

Annabel Christmas (12)
Madeley High School, Crewe

Gok

Gok is the fashion
With all his passion.
Gok, the lookout
He's around and about.
Gok on the telly,
Sorts out big bellies
And that's what it's all about.
Gok's fashion fix,
He loves the chicks!

Zoe Jackson (12)
Madeley High School, Crewe

Inspiration Runs Through The Family

He means the world to me,
Even though he grabs my feet in the morning,
Sending me screaming to my mum.

He works incredibly hard,
So me and Mum can go and see the world,
And he even goes shopping (which he hates).

When me and Mum fight,
He tries to be fair,
So that the war will end.

When I was younger,
We used to play hide-and-seek,
But now we are more grown up,
We annoy Mum instead.

I love him unconditionally,
He inspires me,
He is my dad.

My mum says that I inspire her sometimes,
I guess it runs in the family.

Emily Kettlewell (13)
Madeley High School, Crewe

Loopy Lu

Lucy is great, the best,
Her clothes, shoes and her make-up.
Even though she can be a pest
Planning to get a new pup.
She's amazing, full of laughs,
She's always happy but has her ups and downs.
Although she helps me with my maths,
Always has a smile and no frowns.

She's the best.

Kate Berrisford (13)
Madeley High School, Crewe

My Inspiration

She can slide, she can jive,
She can pump, she can jump,
She can move to the groove
And twirl and swirl.

The music gives her beat,
And she taps her feet.
The sarcasm comes out,
As she dances about.

The hip hop gives her pop,
As she starts to lock.
The pants give her dance
And she starts to prance.

Adrenalin rushes through my veins,
As she starts to gain the strain.
The crowd goes wild,
As she has the style.

Kay is brill
As she starts to thrill.

Jessica Brereton (13)
Madeley High School, Crewe

My Inspiration

That feeling inside, when you feel complete,
When they pop and they slide, move to the beat.
As the music pumps and they start to dance,
And they add an extra move when they have a chance.
When they fly through the air and own the stage,
And all of the audience are engaged.
You just can't help it but you want to move
You long to get involved, get into the groove.
They take a final bow and we all applaud
I love to dance, because you never get bored.

Lydia Griffiths (12)
Madeley High School, Crewe

Hard Or Easy - Inspiration

Brother, mother,
Sportsmen, casts,
Singer, artist, hot dog man,
Inspiration, hard or easy,
Anywhere, anyone,
Can it,
Can't it,
Come,
Come to your mind.
Inspiration hard to find.
It's only hard in your mind.
Break the wall,
Push the barrier,
Be creative,
Push your mind,
Inspiration you will find,
Inspiration.
Easy.
Easy to find.

Shaun Dicks (13)
Madeley High School, Crewe

The Thing

The thing scuttles along the ground,
As quiet as a mouse,
As agile as a leopard.
Its bait is oblivious to it,
It sneaks up ready to pounce,
Its mouth can already taste it.

Snap!
The beautiful taste will have to wait,
Its escape will have to be great,
As it is the bait.

Dan Brown (12)
Madeley High School, Crewe

94

One Man Can Conquer

I seem to stand alone, to conquer all Man's fears,
With eyes open to sadness,
The end is drawing near.
A picture visioned in space
A task set on Mars
My dream just an image
Of a painting full of stars.
I believe in happiness,
A world of joy and light,
An Earth with no pain,
Where trees bloom at night.
I want to see the sunrise,
I wish to see the rain,
Release all fright's darkness,
Cancel out all Earth's vein.
This planet of dead beliefs,
This space of graves and names,
Will rise from the ashes,
One man deleting all of Man's pain.

Jake Lipiec (14)
Madeley High School, Crewe

Simon Dumont

Simon Dumont is the best,
He has a double-front flip Superman up his vest
Here comes The Dumont travelling down west.

The Dew Tour and X-games is his thing,
Here comes The Dumont with all his head bling,
You want his autograph? Give him a ring.

Out in Sweden with the king of after bang,
A jib sesh with the gang,
Skiing in the streets, the police want us hung.

Rowan Emery (13)
Madeley High School, Crewe

Ronaldo . . .

He's unbelievable, he's an inspiration,
He's got skill that we've never seen before,
He'll work on his skill until he's sure
He's definitely the fans' favourite!

Match day arrives, more nervous than ever,
He gets the ball and takes player by player in every stride,
He surely has some pride . . .

He got taken down by a nasty tackle in the penalty box
The penalty was awarded
Standing there, staring at the goalie's eyes
Thinking which way to shoot . . .
Top corner!

Bang!
He goes and celebrates with the fans,
He leaves the opposition like a bunch of cans.

He's definitely my favourite
Player . . .

Thomas Hedley (13)
Madeley High School, Crewe

A Golden Sky

Everyone has a dream
dreams of golden skies and light beams

To live the life you want to
to soar through the night skies
to drop down past the cliffs of Dover
and through the fields of green

Then stop with the winds
stop and shut your eyes
and lean back and fall
Fall for all eternity.

George Edwards (13)
Madeley High School, Crewe

My Inspiration

Becky is an amazing rider who loves horses.
She is good at eventing.
She works with horses every day.
Day in,
Day out,
She helps me understand.
Considerate in every way.
You are guaranteed a laugh
And she makes working with her fun.
She inspires me to ride like she does.
She makes me want to be kind,
A helpful person.
Becky is brave,
She will get on the wildest horses
Then turn them around.
Calm and placid.
My inspiration,
Becky Hartley.

Elizabeth Fox (13)
Madeley High School, Crewe

Wayne Rooney

W inger
A ggressive
Y ellow boots
N o pleasing
E ven has a Porsche Boxster!

R uns fast
O ptimistic
O wn goals
N ever defends
E legant
Y ellow cards.

Tom Egginton (13)
Madeley High School, Crewe

Soaring Through The Sky

I had a dream
I was soaring through the sky
Like a golden eagle
It's a fairy tale
A world where you can't fail
Just close your eyes
And fly away
Through the open bay
Flying up high
Over forests and streams
Looking at the people down below
Up and up through the clouds
Soaring through the sky
This is where I want to be
Knowing I will soon die
In the shimmering
Blue sky
For evermore.

Robyn Lipiec (13)
Madeley High School, Crewe

Pollution Poem!

Pick it up!
Put it in the bin!
That's right, let the environment win!
Come on now, keep Earth clean!
It's the main living machine.

Pollution kills you and me!
Pollution makes us all unhappy.
Why not try to stop driving the car.
Walk to places near and far.
Earth pulls all together as one big community!
Don't let it break us up!

Earle Veitch (12)
Madeley High School, Crewe

Mickey Mouse

M stands for *mouse*

I stands for *icky*. He's not any old icky mouse.

C stands for *cheese*. He's not bothered by cheese like other mice he eats human food instead.

K stands or *keeno*. He's a keeno if you think about it.

E stands for *ears*. His ears are his trademark. Where would he be without them.

Y stands for *yellow*. His noble dog by his side. Pluto even had a planet named after him.

M stands for *Minnie*, his life-long girlfriend. No wonder she loves him. His facial cream makes him younger, he never ages.

O stands for *obvious*. The end is always obvious but it's Disney.

U stands for *underdog*. He's never bigger or stronger or even scarier than his enemies but he still wins.

S stands for *small*, he's always smaller than the rest, but bigger than a mouse.

E stands for *ever*. He's always here and always will be.

James Davies (13)
Madeley High School, Crewe

Help

Time is running out for all,
The animal kingdom is starting to fall.

But we can help, we can act
The only ones and that's a fact.

And still we're the ones
Who bit by bit, blow by blow
Hit by hit.

But here on Earth
It's where we live
So let's try, try to
Protect it.

Clara Ziegler (13)
Madeley High School, Crewe

99

Oh That Bully

Oh that bully
His name's Matthew Wooly
I try to mould my gum shield on the moulder
He just gives me a cold shoulder
As he walks through the school gates
I start to get the shakes
I try to tell
But he would send me straight to Hell.

Oh that bully
His name's Matthew Wooly
He throws my retainer away
Into a container
He punches me in the stomach
I groan
He says I moan.
Oh that bully
His name's Matthew Wooly.

Louie Powell (12)
Madeley High School, Crewe

My Inspiration

My inspiration is my uncle.

He's brave and strong and fights for our country.
When he comes home, he sees us all,
Laughs and plays all day long,
Trusts and gives us good advice.

But when he goes back, we miss him dearly.
I hang a picture on my wall
To never forget him when he's gone
He stays with us all.

He, as you'd say, is my hero,
For what he does for us and for me.

Nicol Jefferies (13)
Madeley High School, Crewe

I Have A Dream

I have a dream that everyone will live,
I have a dream that everyone will give,
All the world together
As happy as a feather.

I have a dream that romance will fall,
I have a dream I'll be caught through it all,
Everyone will smile,
Life will be worthwhile.

I have a dream that the world will all share,
I have a dream that the people will care,
The children will laugh
One world, one path.

I had a dream and it all came true,
I had a dream and the sky turned blue,
I had a dream that tunes would be played,
I had a dream but reality stayed.

Helena Nicklin (13)
Madeley High School, Crewe

Don't Quit

When things go wrong as they sometimes will
When the road you're taking seems all uphill
When the funds are low and the debts are high
And you want to smile, but you have a sigh
When care is pressing you down a bit
Rest if you must, but don't you quit.

Success is failure turned inside out
The silver tint of the clouds of doubt
And you can never tell how close you are
It may be near when it seems afar
So, stick to the fight when you're hard hit -
It's when things go wrong that you mustn't quit.

Jordan Roberts (14)
Madeley High School, Crewe

Cruelty To Animals!

Animals have feelings,
Like any other living things.
Sometimes people know what they have done,
And they do it just for fun.

Nothing should get abandoned,
Or not get loved.
Everyone and everything,
Lives just only once.

Animals get hurt nearly every day,
Their lives after that are sad and grey.
Animals always need love, care and attention,
Oh and did I mention . . .

Cruelty to animals,
I think should stop.
So if you ever see it,
Call a cop!

Jessica Burley (11)
Madeley High School, Crewe

My Inspiration

Dad,
You're always there for me
You always make me smile
You have had some hard times lately
But I'm glad to say you're still here
All the while and going to be OK
But everywhere and anywhere, you're going to be there
And always in my sight through all the day and night.

When you stand before me
You make me jump and say,
I'm glad you're with me Dad,
Every single day!

Abby Shropshire (13)
Madeley High School, Crewe

My Sister

She's pretty,
She's witty,
She's smart,
She likes to drive a cart.

We are family,
Sometimes I have to leave her be,
Uni in September
I will always remember.

She could be white or black,
The love wouldn't lack,
She could be fat or thin,
I'd never throw her in the bin.

She believes,
And she achieves,
She's sound
Like a pound.

Becky Machin (13)
Madeley High School, Crewe

Roald Dahl

Roald Dahl wrote books
All about the world
But most were just about
Strange and loopy stuff.

He wrote about giants
And how they ate children.

He wrote about peaches
That grew to a massive size.

He wrote about children
With magical fingers
And foxes that stole a lot.

Samuel J Lloyd (13)
Madeley High School, Crewe

Wayne Rooney

Rooney is a player who stands tall;
He really concentrates on how he hits the ball.

Rooney has brilliant accuracy and skill;
I'm sure that helps him to pay the bill.

Rooney knows how to work the crowd;
He'll work hard to make Fergie proud.

Rooney wears the Man United top;
But to make sure he stays fit, he'll stay off the pop

Rooney has a lot of guts;
The way he hits the ball, you'd think he was nuts.

He's got talent, he's got speed;
Like a monster you need to feed.

He does it because he can;
That's why I think Rooney's the man.

Raife Plant (13)
Madeley High School, Crewe

Wonderland

I used to stay alone,
Sometimes looking at the stars,
Free of the sounds of moans,
Looking at Jupiter and Mars,
I see the blossomed flowers,
With the breeze in my face,
I stay there seconds, minutes, hours,
With nothing on my case
I see the rabbits hopping two by two,
Everything is peaceful,
They haven't got a clue,
That I am in my dream world,
But keep that, to me and you.

Joshua Bott (12)
Madeley High School, Crewe

Invisible Children

Who knows how long I have been here?
But every day I shed a tear.
Even though I know some day,
Somebody will find a way
To break out of this evil place,
I hope this isn't a hopeless case.
So much pain and so much fear,
All they do is laugh and sneer.

Joseph Kony passes by,
He made those children weep and cry.
Even though they tried and tried,
Kony won and they all died.
But every day I pray and hope,
That I will never ever provoke,
And somebody will come and save,
The children who have been so brave.

Elizabeth Courthold (12)
Madeley High School, Crewe

My Sister Jenny

My sister Jenny
is caring and kind,
always trying to help
to root the happiness that she always finds.

My sister Jenny
has long, straight hair,
she's pretty, she's smart,
she always tries to be fair.

My sister Jenny,
is great in her own way,
she makes me happy and makes me laugh,
I'm glad I can see her every day.

Emily Hadfield (12)
Madeley High School, Crewe

105

Cristiano Ronaldo

C rossing
R unning
I diotic
S kills
T ackles
I ntelligent
A nger
N o defensive ability
O range boots

R ed card
O ver-dramatic
N obody can tackle him
A rgumentative
L ikes running at defenders
D iver
O ptimistic.

Tom Connor (13)
Madeley High School, Crewe

A Grim Fate

To our British heroes, I extend my gratitude,
Thank you for keeping Britain free,
The fall of the Nazis you pursued,
So we remember those who died for us on land and sea.

All of the great battles you did fight,
You shot Germans, but lost your mates,
Despite this you fought day and night,
Because of this you sealed their fates.

For those who died we remember,
For those who laid down their lives,
We remember on a Sunday in November,
We feel sorry for those who never had wives.

Thomas Kendrick (13)
Madeley High School, Crewe

I Have A Dream

I think it would be cool,
If we all could quit school,
For all you sweet tooths you can rely,
On our everlasting chocolate supply,
Being careful and cautious, why?
Especially now you can never die,
With our power we can fly,
Fly until we touch the sky,
It will always be sunny,
Shining on our trees of money,
There will always be fashion,
For people with passion,
I think it would be fair,
If we could all share,
This dream of mine,
It will be divine.

Bronwen Tindsley (14)
Madeley High School, Crewe

I Have A Dream

I have a dream of Man United getting relegated
When they did we all celebrated.
When I score a goal
I will feel great and happy
People shouting my name
I'd never feel ashamed.

When there is no school
I will be in the pool.

Drink when you're eleven
I will be in the pub
Every night and day
Hip hip hooray!

Joe Ashton (14)
Madeley High School, Crewe

Lisa?

She buys me things,
She cheers me up,
Who is she?

She tells me to be brave,
She says it will be okay,
Who can it be?

She takes me places,
She says, 'Never give up!'
Please, who is it?

She's always there for me,
She's brought me up,
She does things for me,
Who is she?

It's my mum!

Eleasha Baddeley (12)
Madeley High School, Crewe

My Inspiration - The Army

Soldiers march one by one,
Soldiers are fearless and also tearless,
They use guns when they get funds,
They use bombs to try and win a war,
That's not against the law.

The terror they face,
Knowing what they have to embrace,
The families they leave,
It must cause a lot of grief,
You can't think of the pain,
As every day we take it in vain.

So here's to the army - if I may
Congratulate them on their hard work to the present day.

Demi Adelburgh (12)
Madeley High School, Crewe

Jenson Button

The race track stands clear
The lights start to glow,
The race draws near
Ready, steady, go!

Brawn's number one
Into the lead
Around the first corner
He starts to pick up speed.

Last lap, last lap
It's going to be tight
Past the chequered flag
Jenson wins again
Another win for him.

Capture the dream.

William Richardson (13)
Madeley High School, Crewe

Robert Sullivan

When I stand there in a line
With belts of all colours at my side,
As I approach grade number nine
In this man I hope to confide.

He's trained in Karate for forty years plus
In 2001 he reached 7th Dan
He achieved it all without making a fuss
And his name is Robert Sullivan.

He wasn't exactly a whiz at school,
But when I'm faced with a hard test
I realise that he was no fool
For not giving up and trying his best.

Elliot Bishop (13)
Madeley High School, Crewe

Maureen

My next-door neighbour
She might be
She still looked after
And cared for me.

She had a dog
Fluffy it was
Although it barked
Every day love it, I did.

We played in the park
Even in the rain
And now she's gone
Oh how I do feel the pain.

Danielle Riley (13)
Madeley High School, Crewe

Shaun White

Flying high above the half-pipe
Snowy whirlwinds in his wake
Cutting through the fluffy powder
Must be a surreal life.

Shaun White is the king of snow -
Godfather of vert
Flipping, spinning, grinding, jibbing, he will never fall.
'Cause Shaun White is the king of snow and he can do it all.

He inspires me to be myself
And do something outdoors.
Shaun White is the person who inspires me
To snowboard.

Jack Nichols (13)
Madeley High School, Crewe

My Feelings For You

I look into your eyes and see blue skies,
I listen to your voice and hear the birds,
I walk past you and feel a breeze,
You are the one for me.

I look into your eyes and see a still river,
I listen to your voice and hear a star,
I walk past you and see a light,
You are the one for me.

I look into your eyes and see a star,
I listen to your voice and hear the wind,
I walk past you and see an image of love,
You are the one for me.

Christian Lawton (12)
Madeley High School, Crewe

The Army

Each day they risk their lives
To help all the people.
To keep them safe.
Their equipment is heavy
But they keep going.
The discipline is tight
But they keep marching on.
Their job is dangerous,
They must be brave.
For truly I am inspired
By the army,
Today, tomorrow and always.

Charlotte Neath (13)
Madeley High School, Crewe

I Have A Dream

I have a dream that one day everyone will be equal,
No one will live in a place where even a drop of water is worshipped,
The rich and famous would have more respect.

No one would walk down the street
And be ashamed of who they are
People would be happy
And wars would be a thing of the past.

Everybody would be treated right,
Everybody would feel good,
This, I hope, one day will be real,
I have a dream.

Katie Beech (12)
Madeley High School, Crewe

My Uncle Inspires Me

Flying into a war zone
In a mighty plane
Nearly getting blown to bits

And coming back in one piece
To his air force base
Taking me on holiday

That's my uncle
That's my uncle
That's my uncle!

Tom Pattinson (12)
Madeley High School, Crewe

Alex Falon

Alex inspires me
She's much softer than she pretends to be.
And when she cried she came to me
And found out how cruel life could be.

When death snatched her sister
She still carried on as she said she would
Even when things got rough
Our Alex stayed tough.

Alex inspires me.

Danielle Riley (13)
Madeley High School, Crewe

My Inspiration

A sports player,
A loving person,
A goal achiever,
A medal winner,
A great helper,
A spirit bringer,
A caring brother,
A good friend
And my inspiration.

Harriet Roberts (13)
Madeley High School, Crewe

Pollution

P lease put your litter in the bin where it belongs.

O nly using small amounts of electricity can make a big difference.

L itter causes pollution, which causes global warming. Do you want that?

L ittle things like recycling can make a difference in the world.

U tterly large holes are forming in the ozone layer. Do you want that?

T housands of people waste electricity and money each day!

I believe that we can keep the planet alive for good.

O nly small things can make a massive difference.

N o one has an excuse, everyone must help.

George Webb (12)
Madeley High School, Crewe

Who Inspires Me - Mum

The person who inspires me is Mum
She is so much fun
And the best thing is that she's my mum.
She can cook
And she clears up the muck,
And the best thing is that she's my mum.
She cares
And helps me with my nightmares,
And the best thing is that she's my mum.

Ryland Bull (12)
Madeley High School, Crewe

My Inspiration

My inspiration is my mum
Because she is pretty and smart.
She is a doctor beautician
This is a good job, isn't it?
I love her and for this matter
I love her more than anything in the universe.
I she wouldn't be, I wouldn't be
So I thank everything for her
And the things she's made for me.

Katalin Nagy (12)
Madeley High School, Crewe

God

Almighty God, You rule our world
You made us from a giant swirl
We pledge ourselves with all our hearts
And You made us Your piece of art
We killed Your Son on a Cross
But You're still our almighty boss.

Oliver Hosler-Ruxton (13)
Madeley High School, Crewe

Pollution

P eople all over the world polluting
O nly we can stop this
L ove the world like it loves us
L et this world live in a clean environment
U nder the skin of this world it wants clean
T ake time to think about what you are doing
I n the world everyone can help
O ver time you need to help the world
N othing other than us can stop pollution.

Elsbeth Massey (12)
Madeley High School, Crewe

I Have A Dream

My dream, my dream, my dream
I dream of a world where there's no fights at night
A world where there's rights and responsibilities
A world with love without hatred

My dream, my dream, my dream
I dream of a place not far from here
A place where gentle snowfalls
A place of teamwork to make a snowman

My dream, my dream, my dream
A school where they don't judge you
A school that takes you for who you are
A school with no popular people or geeks, where we're all the same

My dream, my dream, my dream
I dream that I can help those in need
I dream that we all give and not take
I dream
That all are gentle, kind and calm.

Charlotte Stewart (13)
Maple Hayes Hall School, Lichfield

I Have A Dream

I have a dream
Which doesn't want to come true
It almost seems impossible
I don't know what to do

I've thought of every thought
I've pulled on every string
I don't know what to think of
Bells just don't seem to ring

A part of me wants to keep going
A part of me wants to stop
But I want to keep climbing
Until I reach the top

It may take the rest of my life
It may even kill me
But if I am to succeed this dream
For life it will fulfil me.

Roddy Lynch (13)
Maple Hayes Hall School, Lichfield

I Have A Dream

I have a dream
A terrible one which lives inside me
I don't want anyone to see

It gives me sickening thoughts
All I want to do is forget
This dreadful thing that I regret

I've got to break the ice
And then maybe my dreams can be nice
I've got to destroy this dream

Why won't it go?
I have to know.

Tom Abbotts (13)
Maple Hayes Hall School, Lichfield

Spare A Thought For Me

You go home and have your tea, but would you spare a
thought for me?
You go out and have a ball, while my life starts to fall.
You go to school and moan and cheek, but my thoughts I'm afraid
to speak.
You play games like jump rope, I lie on the floor, my ribs are broke.
You can see the clouds today, but I have been locked away.
My dream is to be just like you, I want a mom and dad that
love me too,
So if I can ask one thing before I go,
Will you spare a thought for me next time you eat your tea?

Lauren Nokes (13)
Maple Hayes Hall School, Lichfield

I Have A Dream

I have a dream
to dash and dart around the galaxy
to become an explorer and swing with my friends the apes
to meet a dinosaur and take it home and put it under my bed
to twist and twirl like my friend, the ballet dancer
to jump and gallop through the fields on a noble steed
to twist and twirl on water like a figure skater on ice
to know the secrets of the universe like a bear knows the ways of the woods
to lounge on mountains of gold
to live forever and ever to do these things again.

Chloe Johnson (14)
Maple Hayes Hall School, Lichfield

I Have A Dream

Imagine
Going full speed down and down
Imagine
Hitting a ramp while going faster and faster
Imagine
The next thing you know you are soaring through the sky
Imagine
You are going up and up like a bird
Imagine
You are the bird.

Adam Homer (13)
Maple Hayes Hall School, Lichfield

A Dream?

You talk of a dream world,
A place where

People are dying from malnutrition,
Children are screaming from the terror of bombs,
Girls are being raped nightly,
Bullets whizz by as husbands go to work,
A best friend just dies in front of you at war,
Is it a dream?

I call it a *nightmare!*

Alan Woodall (14)
Maple Hayes Hall School, Lichfield

This Is Just A Dream

I have a dream

That I walk on water
With skill and style
I play and dance on waves that
Never sink.

Rebecca Speed (14)
Maple Hayes Hall School, Lichfield

I Have A Dream

I have a dream for all mankind.
To better us all,
To bring fruit from the vine,
To bring us all to unity,
To sail on the eternal seas.

The journey will be hard that's true,
But it is all down to you.

David Lewis (14)
Maple Hayes Hall School, Lichfield

I Had A Dream

I had a dream
That I was in a game
Not just any game but the game
'Call of Duty: World at War'
The best game in the world
I was on the front line
Ship at night
Screams of my fellow men I left behind
I wish it was a dream but sadly it's wasn't.

William Makin (13)
Maple Hayes Hall School, Lichfield

My Dream Is . . .

To be rich and famous, wear gowns like gold
Be able to buy items that are there to be sold
To dine with the Queen and always be seen
To sit in the carriage and imagine I was at the Queen's marriage

That's my dream.

Georgina Burrow (14)
Maple Hayes Hall School, Lichfield

I Have A Dream

I dream of lots of theme parks
Filled with very fast rides
Just children and open all the time
It will be free.

There will be no school

I dream of living in a place like New York
Where it's modern and bigger with lots more shops
It's not like England, small and very dull.

Sean Bridges (14)
Maple Hayes Hall School, Lichfield

I Dream . . .

I could be in a band and live on the sea,
Sail the seas, me and me mateys
Be a marine engineer, oily and greasy.
Play my guitar, 'Bohemian Rhapsody'.
This is my dream,
One day it will come true.

Kole Judge (13)
Maple Hayes Hall School, Lichfield

Alone - Bullying

I sit in the playground
I sit there all alone
no friends to play with
I can't wait to go home.

They constantly judge me
when nobody's near
call me names, hit me
I'm so full of rage and fear.

My parents ask me what's wrong
but I just sit in dead silence
they know something's not right
they don't believe violence.

I'm scared, really scared
what will happen if I tell?
They just won't stop bullying me
my life always feels like hell.

What would you do to stop this?
When you run home, crying in despair
not one word to your family
why is life just so unfair?

When I walk to school in the morning
I hear loud footsteps behind
I try to walk faster
I get flashbacks in my mind.

I look in the mirror at night
and think maybe they're right
it hurts me inside
look at me, I really am a sight.

They push me into corners
hit me with anything they can find
I thought it was a nightmare
I could not see, I thought I was blind.

Every day things just get worse
my parents know something's wrong
I have bruises covering my body

this has been going on for so long.

I still don't say a word
I feel like it's all my fault
my appearance, my character maybe
why won't it all come to a halt?

I think it's time to stop this
please help me, I can't cope anymore
I know I have something left in me
that's it, no more suffering, no more.

Lucy Hodson (14)
Prince Henry's High School, Evesham

A Dream Of Peace

I had a dream about a world,
A world that's now at peace,
Guns and knives and khaki suits,
All thrown down in the streets.

The people were rejoicing,
And yelling out with glee,
The men were all lining up,
To sign the peace treaty.

I had a dream about a world,
A world that's now at peace,
Guns and knives and khaki suits,
All thrown down in the streets.

The brass band was playing,
A happy, peaceful song,
People stood hand in hand,
In peaceful harmony.

I had a dream about a world,
A world that's now at peace,
Guns and knives and khaki suits,
All thrown down in the streets.

Thomas Walkeden (13)
Prince Henry's High School, Evesham

Still, She Makes Me Smile

Ill from very young, tired all the time.
Not much time for friends,
Her mother kept her in.
Still, tried her best at school
But wasn't there enough.
Got moved down a year
She was teased for being 'dumb'.

Then I met her for the very first time
So pretty, so nice, how could she be teased.
We hung out a lot and she started to get better
She'd been through so much
I didn't want to let her down
So I stood up for her and stayed by her side
Even if I knew it would leave me with no one but her
She was all I needed
My best friend
She did make me smile.

We became so close,
She'd nearly got through her illness
But then came her scar,
She couldn't live with it
She begged for surgery but it was too expensive
She was teased once more
I felt so sorry
She would cry every night,
She would wish she was dead
But still on her good days,
She always made me smile.

Soon after she gained another illness
This time worse.
I would sit with her
She would tell me of her pain.
I wanted to help, but knew there was nothing I could do.
A couple of months after we managed to have more fun
She would try and forget the pain just to be with me
She really was incredible
And always made me smile

Even when she was at her worst.

Just last year she managed to get through everything
She's now ready for college
And is as happy as ever
She inspires me in everything she does
She really is my best friend
And still she makes me smile.

Victoria Horne (14)
Prince Henry's High School, Evesham

Mum, You Inspire Me!

My mum is who inspires me,
because of all the things she does,
like when she does the washing up,
she always wears her gloves.

When my mum got bullied at school,
because of her epilepsy,
she was strong and tough,
to tell them they weren't cool.

I love my mum because of how
she can cope with things,
she's an angel to me
that has wings.

She makes me smile when I'm sad
and she never thinks about herself
but always about others,
which sometimes makes me mad.

I want to be like my mum,
because she copes with things
and never lets them interfere.
Mum you inspire me!

So that is why my mum inspires me
she always does her best.

Charlotte Kelson (13)
Prince Henry's High School, Evesham

Time To Realise

It's been three years now,
I can't stand the pain.
I've been bullied my whole life,
It's driving me insane.

They constantly tease me
And treat me like dirt.
I just can't cope anymore,
How much can one person hurt?

I've never really had friends
And my parents don't care.
What shall I do now?
Life's just so unfair.

People stand and watch,
As they hit me to the ground.
Bruises all over my body,
I still don't make a sound.

It can't be a nightmare
As I sit and cry every night.
Staring into the distant stars,
My body full of fright.

All I want is some help,
I have no one to talk to.
I just can't hide this;
It's too much to go through.

Bruises, cuts, scars and blood,
I look such a mess.
I cannot help but breakdown,
I can't cope with the stress.

Please give me a break
And help me through this.
I don't want to be here,
Those goods times I miss.

I've never really been shown,
What good times are all about.
I've been bullied since a young age,

126

Many feelings I've never felt.

As I slowly start to realise,
I could make my life fine.
I have to sort this out,
It's time to ring Childline.

Millie Evans (14)
Prince Henry's High School, Evesham

Day Before War

D on't waste the last day of peace
A s once the battle starts
Y our war has begun and the words ringing in your ear are
'Never surrender!'

B arrels flashing, noise deafening, enemy approaching - 'Never surrender!'
E choing in your ears are the sounds of screams, all hell breaks
lose it seems - but 'Never surrender!'
F lashing before your eyes plays a sight of horror to accompany
the screams - 'Never surrender!'
O vercoming every obstacle crushing everything in your way fighting,
winning, losing - 'Never surrender!'
R uining your life, your mental health bruising - 'Never surrender!'
E xciting, the barrels' bullets fly, the very last stand, one side will win, the
other die - 'Never surrender!'

W ar is at hand but drawing to a close, when peace will come nobody
knows. 'Never surrender!'
A broken landscape and lives are the cost, to fight for your reasons and
'Never surrender!'
R isen to victory, you hold your head high, but when you look around you
try not to cry.

Remember
'Never surrender.'

      But maybe it's time
      We all surrendered!

Tom Cook (13)
Prince Henry's High School, Evesham

Loneliness

Sitting alone on the edge of the bench,
Watching every other person
Having fun with their friends,
Not one looks at me with a smile,
Just a face that says,
'Look at that scum on the bench.'
Even kids with braces have
Friends.
Everyone but me.

Mother asks every evening,
'Everything okay at school?'
I force a smile and nod
But it's not, nothing is.

I want to be home,
In my room.
At least when I'm home and alone
I don't feel like an outsider.
School's a different story.

Pushed about in the playground
Or locker room
Seriously
Does that sound like fun to you?
Being picked last in school sports.
Just imagine it.
No one joining you for lunch.
You may go out every weekend,
I don't.

That was all a while ago now
Everything's been forgotten.
I'm picked in school teams,
I eat with a friend at lunch.
She sticks up for me too,
When they do bully me.

Jessamie Klaiber (13)
Prince Henry's High School, Evesham

Inspirational Poetry

My heart is cold
My love is broken
And now I'm smoken
I saw you on 'Dukes of Hazards'
I saw you on TV
I saw you on E4
Of that I'm sure
She smiled at me through the screen
She was with another man
His name was Sam
Oh damn
Not Sam
But now my love is free
We were meant to be
Jessica Simpson and me
I saw her through the glass
Far away
I gazed at her
Through the glass
Don't know how much time had past
But it feels like forever
I was submerged in love
That is true
I was left in the corner like a pile of poo
Oh it made me mad
But I couldn't react
I was stuck between the glass
I must survive
With her love
I am strong
I must survive
Oh.

Tom Palmer (14)
Prince Henry's High School, Evesham

The Bully

Skies in my life are always grey,
All because of something you say,
You make me believe I am worthless,
All because of *you*, the bully.

I try to avoid you, stay away,
You threaten me, dare I tell?
I have no choice, I am cornered,
All because of *you*, the bully.

At school I put on a brave face,
But when I get home I cower and cry,
I don't know why I bother with life,
All because of *you*, the bully.

When I go home, I think it's all over,
I check my phone, there you are again,
I drown my sorrows, and wish there was no tomorrow,
All because of *you*, the bully.

But I know that I must be strong,
To overcome this terrible nightmare,
Things start to brighten up,
All because of *you*, the bully,

I now know, I must make a stand,
Ignore your feeble attempts to dishearten me,
Become a stronger person out of this,
All because of *you*, the bully.

I now realise, I am not worthless,
You were no better than I was,
I am now the strongest anyone can be,
I thank you, and pity you, the bully.

Harry Parker (13)
Prince Henry's High School, Evesham

We Have Freedom

The fight for freedom,
We need to lead them,
Through the south,
Stop the mouth,
Of all the anti,
There is no sanity,
Of the people,
There is nothing equal,
Where is the sequel?
We fight the freedom.

We shall take the power back,
There is no time to lack,
More time to attack,
The movement in motion,
We're in the right light,
Study for an insight,
We lost the culture,
The culture lost,
Now we take it back.
Everyone fight the freedom.

The present curriculum,
I put my fist in them,
We need to have a dream,
Get on the regime,
Rise upon,
We can live on,
Keep the 'inferior,'
Less mass hysteria,
Now we have the freedom.

Matt Neal (14)
Prince Henry's High School, Evesham

Inspiration

I give ideas,
When people have none.
I help people flourish,
When they're falling behind.
I bring people up,
When they crash down.
I give people hope,
When all they see is black.
I help people through,
Some of the toughest times.
I like people to feel,
Like there is a way out.
I show them the light,
When they reach their lowest point.
I helped to make,
Some magnificent places.
I helped you through,
When you needed me most.
When you needed that hope,
I helped you.
When the going gets tough,
I'll stand by your side.
When you ask for me,
I will be there.
And when you're upset,
I make you smile again.
I do all this out of the goodness of my heart.

I am *inspiration.*

Carenza Barnett (14) & Ellie Gregory
Prince Henry's High School, Evesham

Homelessness

Sitting on the pavement,
In the pouring rain,
Really, really cold,
Want to go inside.

Haven't got any food,
Need something to eat,
Haven't got any money,
I need some now.

Trying to beg for some money,
No one giving any to me,
I've got to get some money,
Don't know how.

Every night I sleep on the bench,
On the edge of the park,
Surviving only on clothes,
Can't get to sleep.

Always really tired,
Never know what to do,
Just try to get some money,
That spend it all on food.

Some day I wish someone would come
And give me some money
Or give me a sheltered place to sleep at night,
Somewhere warm.
Will you pass me by?

Lauren Tucker (13)
Prince Henry's High School, Evesham

133

Inspiration

Inspiration comes in many shapes and forms,
through bravery, love and those we come to mourn.

On the sandy dunes of the battle map,
comrades, friendship, they all feel trapped.
Sent to battle by a country worn,
through war, destruction, the country is torn.

Now up the ladder to the building that burns,
there's not a moment when hearts will turn.

A father's wish with his last long breath,
'Live long my son, don't fear death.
Be strong, be free,
I'm always with thee.'

Through pain, through torture,
in sight and mind,
hearing and love, thee will not find.

These men, these women,
strong and brave,
their love, their passion,
I so long crave.

For these are the people who inspire me most,
strong, brave, loving and free from coast to coast.

Ellis Tustin (14)
Prince Henry's High School, Evesham

My Family

My parents are people, people that always care,
They comfort us when we are sad,
But tell us off when we are bad,
When we have a problem they help to sort it out,
And they reassure us when we have a doubt,
And they will always be there.

Ellie Bolland (14)
Prince Henry's High School, Evesham

134

Bullying

Why me? What have I done?
I am just a normal person
Just like everyone else
Well, I think so!

Sometimes people are born with a disability
It's not their fault or mine
I was starved of oxygen when I was born
And therefore I have a walking disability.

Everyone is different, everyone should
Respect each other for what they are
But Jess did not
Jess is a big bully.

She would call me names
And make me feel bad
'Sticks and stones can hurt my bones
But words cannot hurt me.'

That saying is so wrong
Words are very powerful and meaningful
Do something about it
Things can only get better.

It will stop if you tell someone!

Charlotte Arthur (14)
Prince Henry's High School, Evesham

Going Forward

Progressing together may take time
Working together can inspire the mind
Striving, achieving to reach your goal
Nothing is impossible.

Callum McOmish (14)
Prince Henry's High School, Evesham

Abusive

It started off funny,
but then it got bad,
I became extremely sad,
the words came at me,
so fast,
I just wish it was in the past,
it makes me feel so alone,
just waiting for someone to phone.

I sit here silent and still,
just waiting for that man to come back,
he scares me until I crack.
He took my V,
then beat me up,
I was unwillingly stuck,
crying for hours on end,
it's just me to fend.

One day, everything changed,
for better or worse I couldn't explain,
but something inside of me had ended,
I could stop pretending.
A year to the day I'd been gone,
I was finally done.

Lauren McWilliams (14)
Prince Henry's High School, Evesham

Keep On Going

Never give up
Even when the clouds are grey
When everything seems impossible
Your spirits are down and the going's tough
When you get knocked about and it,
Seems like your legs won't carry you any further
There is always light shining through a small hole
Always something else left in you
The courage to keep on going no matter what
So get up and go
Don't look back at the pain you've been through
Just hold your head high and focus about what's in front
Anything is possible, there's nothing in your way
As the tunnel comes out at the mountain top
Leaning forward, past the line
Your break the barrier into greatness
Now all that pain and fear seems worthwhile
You can now relax and feel good
Everyone knows that you can achieve your dream
Just go ahead and grab it.

Angus Lamb & Rupert Malein (14)
Prince Henry's High School, Evesham

Parents

P ay attention whenever you brag
A lways there for you in your time of need
R emind you how much they care about you
E ntertain you in your boredom
N ever speak negatively, to make you feel better
T ell them a secret, they keep it
S ay what's wrong and what's right.
     The motto of parents
     You either love them or your hate them!

Hannah Shaw (14)
Prince Henry's High School, Evesham

We Have A Dream

We can do it together
Work as a team
Share it together
Share the dream.

We have a dream
A poem to write
To help us grow
Together we'll fight.

Have you ever thought
Of a peaceful land?
We will try and try again
Take another by the hand.

We believe in helping
Everyone around us
We believe in being
True to ourselves.

Together we can do it
Live the dream.

Emma Kendrick & Alex Gittens (14)
Prince Henry's High School, Evesham

Bill Gates Is Brilliant

Bill Gates is brilliant!
Bill Gates created an operating system at the age of only 15.
Bill Gates is brilliant!
Bill Gates has billions of dollars but gives most of the money to charity.
Bill Gates is brilliant!
Bill Gates has inspired me to learn more about the computer, learn
different languages, build software and website templates.
Bill Gates is brilliant!
Bill Gates makes me believe I can succeed and achieve.
Bill Gates is brilliant!

Sam Hudson (14)
Prince Henry's High School, Evesham

War

Ducking from bombs,
Running for cover,
Shooting at the enemy,
Not one another.

Snipers shooting,
Troops dying,
And all for what?
For someone they have never met,
Saying 'We control this place now.'
Or, 'We have dominated the enemy.'

The commanders I mean,
Sat behind their desks with a crazy dream
Of world domination
Or purging the world of people with a right to live there.

Why do people have a lust for war?
Ending lives and love's no more.
We are all the same
Why do we have war?

Alistair Connell (14)
Prince Henry's High School, Evesham

Bullying

I have a feeling that one day bullying will be just a memory.
That no one, no matter what shape or form
No one will use words like bullets that hurt and wound.

I have a feeling that no one would look down at someone
Or judge people by their appearance like they are a cover of a book.

I have a feeling that one day the one person who bullies and mocks
Will get it hard.
Hard back like a tonne of bricks on their shoulders.

I have a feeling what goes around comes around.

Harry Bulow (14)
Prince Henry's High School, Evesham

Terrorism

I believe in a better tomorrow,
Life without terrorism,
A life without regret or worry.

I believe in world peace,
Where kids don't need to worry,
Where there are no terrorists.

I believe that one day,
The world will stand against
Terrorism and drive it out.

I believe that children
Won't be terrorists and
Will help destroy terrorism.

I believe that there's a
Better world,
A terrorist-free world.

I believe we can drive
Terrorism *out!*

Owen Hatch (14)
Prince Henry's High School, Evesham

Impossible

Impossible is a funny word
Impossible is just a big word
Used by little boys
Impossible is not a fact
It's an opinion
Impossible is not a declaration
It's a dare
Impossible is potential
Impossible is temporary
Impossible is nothing.

Jack Hunston (14)
Prince Henry's High School, Evesham

Inspirational; A Poem

Inspiration; a dream to strive by,
Motivation; actions speak louder than words,
Encouragement; following in the footsteps,
Influence; from others to others.

Discouraged; but never giving up,
Disheartened; but never losing heart.

Impress; and stay humble,
Animate; those around you,
Reassure; those in need,
Believe; in yourself.

Pessimistic; at moments,
Crestfallen; and rise above.

Enliven; the world around you,
Trigger; a change,
Invigorate; and make things happen,
Impassion; and believe in your cause.

Alice Morrey (14)
Prince Henry's High School, Evesham

Inspirational Poetry

Bear Behaving Badly
And laughter.
Runs through everyone's heart
Now we cherish them
Every day for what they do
Young people love them
And take pride in how
Nev makes people jump up and down
Waiting for it to be shown
Now it will be the most enjoyed show ever
And the best
Very funny.

Russell Burke
Prince Henry's High School, Evesham

Gurkhas

Those righteous men
Helped us defeat a greater evil
They suffered great anguish
By defeating Hitler and co.

We pay them back
By refusing them entry into this noble land
We sadly stand by
As people racially abuse them.

A question gets put into my head
Why can't we honour these men
Instead of supporting racist bigots?
If it wasn't for them we would be German.

So now with all of these celebratory days
We need to honour these men
For the good of our country
For the good of our pride.

Will Collett (14)
Prince Henry's High School, Evesham

Martin Luther King

He was a man who stood up for what he believed in,
For a better life for people.
He was a man who did anything to put his point across to the world,
To help those who were miserable.
He was a man who had a dream
That little white children and little black children would hold hands
                                                                    as friends.

Well his dream has come true.
What would the world be like if he hadn't been born?
'I have a dream,' he said those words,
Those words which have changed the world.

Ashley Lingwood (13)
Prince Henry's High School, Evesham

142

I Have A Dream

'I have a dream,'
said Martin Luther King as his dream.
It was a sensible dream
that anyone could dream.
But it wasn't an easy dream
to make it a true dream.
'I have a dream,'
It was a courageous dream
it was also an important dream
that someone should dream
and make it a true dream.
To make it a true dream
it was quite hard, not at all like dreaming.
Finally the dream came true.
Now it's not a dream
and so it inspires me to say that
'I have a dream.'

Maria Mathew (14)
Prince Henry's High School, Evesham

Racism

R acism is unfair and unkind.
A buse shouted at you, walking down the street.
C onstant beatings for your race.
I nsults the kids at school save just for you.
S o alone, you feel separate from all the other kids.
M issing. You think to yourself, if you went missing and
　　never come back, they wouldn't miss you.

Danielle Scarrott (14)
Prince Henry's High School, Evesham

Imagine

Imagine a world full
of peace

Imagine a world where
everyone cares

Imagine a world with
no racism

Imagine a world with
no crime

Imagine a world with
no war

Imagine

Imagine is a small word
that anyone can
run away with.

Ben Harvey (14)
Prince Henry's High School, Evesham

Inspiration

Where can we find it?
When will we need it?
What will it be?
Inspiration comes from within,
Nothing or no one can force it,
It is uncontrollable,
Who needs it?

Lucy Button & Laura Croft (13)
Prince Henry's High School, Evesham

Girls Incomplete

Girls can be shy or the type who say hi,
Selfish or mean, the bitchiest queen,
Blonde or brunette, we're all the same
As words pass our lips, *we don't take the blame.*

Some girls hide their faces with loads of make-up,
So boys think they're prettier.
Why do this?
What's the point?
Why hide your face and keep you head down?

It's not you, don't change yourself for boys' opinions.
Be who you are and they will like you more for who you are.
Phoney acts,
Phoney looks,
It's *all a lie,*
So why judge yourself for someone you're not!

Nichola Brotherton (14)
Prince Henry's High School, Evesham

Dad

My dad is great,
he teaches my to fly fish,
he teaches me to shoot,
he teaches me to drive my car
and helps me fix the boot.

He buys me lots of nice stuff
and gives me lots of money,
he gets very angry and goes off in a huff
and I just think it is very funny.

He's always really fun
and helps me with lots of stuff,
he helps with homework
and always encourages me on.

Toby Williamson (14)
Prince Henry's High School, Evesham

A Girl's Day

Girls have to look gorgeous,
for the sake of boys' opinions.
Girls have to be in with the latest fashion,
for people to appreciate them.
Girls plaster themselves with make-up
to try to look good.
Girls say bad things
to try to look cool,
but c'mon who are you kidding?
It makes them look a fool
being shy or outgoing?
Walking past that boy, or asking him out?
Keep your head high
and stay with your friends,
to be honest, that's the best in life.
This happens in a girl's life every day.

Taylor White (13)
Prince Henry's High School, Evesham

I'm In The Army

Dying for my country
Fight in Afghanistan
Bullets flying everywhere
Every second counts
I'm in the army.

Split second decisions
Life and death
A grenade blows up
Shockwaves through the air
I'm in the army.

Shrapnel hits me back and forth
I go down in pain
My vision blurs
It's gone dark
I was in the army.

George Dudley (14)
Prince Henry's High School, Evesham

Never Give Up - Kate Moss

She may have taken drugs in the past
But that doesn't mean she isn't still inspiring
A lot of things she's done
Like the endless modelling contracts
And her own range of clothes at Top Shop
Starts to make up for the drugs she took.

It started to go downhill for her when the companies found out
They started pulling out of the contracts
She tried and tried to stop for her career
And eventually got back on track
Now the modelling companies have all come running back
She's an inspiration because she never gave up
And she's managed to get back to normal
After everything.

Gabbie Agrusa (13)
Prince Henry's High School, Evesham

Imagine The World Was A Better Place

They leave me here,
In the car.
No open windows or air to breathe,
I've not eaten for five days,
They all forgot to feed me,
Now I'm chained against a post,
With my owner in the distance,
Driving away from me.
They leave me here all through the night,
While the cold wind blows,
I stand here shivering,
I wonder what's gone wrong,
They said they'd always need me,
But now I'm here alone,
I wish the world was a better place and that I could go home.

Emily Watkins (12)
St John's Middle School, Bromsgrove

148

Imagine The World

I'm starving, hungry,
And I need food,
My stomach's rumbling,
And being rude.
I tell it no,
We have no more,
But still I search,
All on the floor.
Imagine the world was a better place,
Without poverty staring us in the face!

Gunshots, more gunshots,
Surrounding me,
I duck, I dive,
And then I flee.
Next I'm staring at a gun,
It's aiming at my head,
The trigger's pulled,
Bang! Bang! Now I'm dead.
Imagine the world was a better place,
Without war staring us in the face!

I'm black,
You're white,
Our skin is different,
But still we fight.
You call me names,
And push me around,
You hide my stuff,
So it can't be found.
Imagine the world was a better place,
Without racism staring us in the face!

Beth Davis (13)
St John's Middle School, Bromsgrove

Imagine The World Was A Better Place

I want peace for the world,
Is that too much to ask?
Some people love war,
They think that it's a task.

Just consider for a moment,
How many get hurt.
Shot dead in a second,
With blood on their shirt.

Bullying people,
Is a part of this too.
Just give a thought to others,
When you've made them feel blue.

Racism is stupid,
If you believe in it you're mad.
Why don't people see,
Being different isn't bad?

Respect should be for everyone,
No matter your religion, or if you're obese.
I'm here to tell you what I feel we need,
A world of nothing but love and peace.

Siobhan Hughes (13)
St John's Middle School, Bromsgrove

Imagine The World Was A Better Place . . .

Imagine the world was a better place,
Where people weren't judged on their race,

Imagine the world with no pollution,
Where we could conjure every solution,

Imagine the world where sinners go to jail,
Until they confess and are released on bail,

Imagine the world where everyone's free,
Without having to beg or plea.

Imagine the world where animals are safe,
Where they can believe in us with faith,

Imagine the world where there is no white or black,
Where we can join together without any crack,

Imagine the world where there isn't a bully,
Where people can live free and fully.

Imagine the world with mountains of food,
Where people can share without being rude,

I hope this poem has solved the case,
Let's make our world a better place!

Emma, Wilson (13)
St John's Middle School, Bromsgrove

Imagine The World Was A Better Place

You see them whining by the roadside
Weak from hunger
Their owners lied
Now they hate the human race
Imagine the world was a better place.

Baby mice take their first breath
But they do not know the wicked future
How they will suffer pain before death
Now they hate the human race
Imagine the world was a better place.

Even monkeys suffer this pain
As they are tested with drugs
Their lives will never be the same
Now they hate the human race
Imagine the world was a better place.

What if the world was run by animal kind?
Would they test on us
Or would they have a peaceful mind?
Would we hate the animal race
Or would the world be a better place?

Emily Catherine Teer (12)
St John's Middle School, Bromsgrove

Imagine The World Was A Better Place

I'm lying on the concrete floor,
My stumped tail aches, so sore.
Tomorrow, my ears and my teeth,
Will be lying in the ground beneath.
With no medicine, or no drugs,
They hit me, cut me; act like thugs,
They just don't care.
It's really not fair.

I'm crushed in the back of an animal truck,
Bleating and baaing, covered in muck.
Taken away from the lush green field,
Like thousands of others, my fate is sealed.
Soon I'll be hanging, my throat bleeding and cut,
No fleece, no limbs, no tail, no gut.
My life is cut short, my suffering is over,
As death grips me.

Imagine the world was a better place,
Where animal cruelty was a thing of the past.
Imagine the world was a better place,
Where animals can live in peace at last.

Alice Evans (12)
St John's Middle School, Bromsgrove

Imagine The World Was A Better Place

Imagine the world was a better place
They'd be no arguments, whatever race.
Imagine the world where war was no more,
And everyone's equal, from rich to poor.

Imagine the world as a better place
Discrimination is a disgrace.
Imagine the world with no pollution
To save the Earth, that's the solution.

Imagine the world was a better place
Where everyone's allowed their own space.
Save the pandas, save the ice caps
And the world will be safe, perhaps.

Imagine the world was a better place
I do every day.
Why can't it be a better place?
Then the world will be here to stay.

Max Banner (13)
St John's Middle School, Bromsgrove

Imagine The World Was A Better Place

Imagine the world was a better place,
No one would fight or care about race.
There would be no war, abuse or crime,
There would be no people in prison doing time.
Children wouldn't be beaten for no reason at all,
Adults would be loving for tall and small.
In this world, not all are bad,
But some still are, it's really quite sad.
Parents are using their defenceless kids,
To take out their anger, or sell them in bids.
This could even end with a murder in hand,
So why can't there be peace across this land?

Robyn Burrell (13)
St John's Middle School, Bromsgrove

154

Imagine The World Was A Better Place

Imagine the world was a better place,
No small animal trapped in a tiny case,
Happy animals wandering the street,
Friendly people you shall meet.

Imagine the world was a better place,
No arguing between the human race,
Vandalism and graffiti would be scarce,
A place where everyone would care.

Imagine the world was a better place,
No food going to waste,
There wouldn't be any starving kids,
Never don'ts but always dids.

Imagine the world was a better place,
No small animal trapped in a tiny case,
Happy animals wandering the street,
Friendly people you shall meet.

Miriam Peters (12)
St John's Middle School, Bromsgrove

Imagine The World Was A Better Place

Imagine the world was a better place,
Where no one would care about your colour or race,
Animal cruelty was out the window,
No one would make someone feel low,
African people would have something to eat,
And have shoes to wear on their feet
Homeless people would have somewhere to live,
And no one would get teased and called a div,
Parents would love and care for their children,
Instead of abusing them and killing them,
Together we can change the world for the best,
So come on and help and don't be a pest!

Charlotte Mitchell (13)
St John's Middle School, Bromsgrove

Imagine The World Was A Better Place

Imagine the world was a better place,
You wouldn't be afraid to show your face.

Imagine you could go out late at night,
You wouldn't have to live in real fright.

Imagine walking down the street,
All the great people you could meet.

Imagine poverty becoming history,
No more deaths and murder mysteries.

Imagine all the animals who are in despair,
Breathing in pollution from the air.

Imagine the world could be less like this,
Lots of respect and replying 'Yes Miss!'

Nicole Murray (13)
St John's Middle School, Bromsgrove

Imagine The World Was A Better Place

Imagine the world was a better place,
Where nobody cares about colour or race.
The rights of life were guaranteed
And we were assured a good day's feed.

Animals would be cared for,
Instead of always feeling sore
Children would believe in their dreams,
Instead of being in the middle of crime scenes.

Third world countries living a good life,
Instead of all the anger and strife.
I would love this world,
What about you?

Chase Pheysey-Hoban (13)
St John's Middle School, Bromsgrove

Imagine The World Was A Better Place

Imagine the world was a better place,
Where no one had the right,
To disgrace,
Creed, race, sexuality,
Why do people wanna' hurt me?

Imagine the world was a better place,
No walls between us,
Just cos of my race,
No pain, no pain,
Just cos of their face.

Imagine the world was a better place,
Can you treat me equally?
Then we can live oh so freely,
Discrimination,
Should go down the station.

Greg Davenport (12)
St John's Middle School, Bromsgrove

Imagine The World Was A Better Place

Imagine the world as a better place,
Where no one is discriminating each other's race,
Except the colour, religion or sexuality,
What is the difference between them and me?
Only if people were equal from rich to poor,
Then there will be no more war,
Discriminating is a disgrace,
It would help if everyone had his or her own space,
Can you treat us equally at least?
With no wall between us to leave us to decrease,
Why can't people agree,
That people like this should have as much freedom as
Me!

Simon Fox (13)
St John's Middle School, Bromsgrove

Imagine The World Was A Better Place

Imagine the world was a better place,
A world where people aren't judged on their race,
A world where people aren't scared to walk home alone,
Where people don't get drunk all the time and raise their tone,
A world where not every argument turns into a court case,
A world where we are not competitive like in one big race.
A world where the right people go to jail,
A world where sinners always fail,
Imagine a world where abuse just isn't there,
A world where everything is just even and fair,
Imagine a world where we find a solution
For the ongoing problem of pollution,
Imagine a world where pets are cared for,
A world where people hold open the door,
To the life that we have learnt to adore.

Amy Jones
St John's Middle School, Bromsgrove

Imagine The World Was A Better Place

Imagine the world was a better place
Where people were not judged for their
Decisions or their race.

Imagine the world was a better place,
Where animals were not used as something to hate.

Imagine a world with every solution,
We could finally stop all of the pollution.

Imagine a world with no crime,
Where people actually did some time.

Imagine a world where pets were cared for,
Instead of being kicked on the floor.
Imagine a world with all of these things,
Life would just be so amazing!

Lily Saville (12)
St John's Middle School, Bromsgrove

158

Imagine The World Was A Better Place

Imagine the world was a better place,
No more danger on the human face:
Less people dying, no people lying,
No more cruelty, seeing children crying.

If only the world were a better place,
No bullies who treat you like bait;
Shouting, screaming, none of that heard,
There will be more peace in the world.

Imagine the world was a better place,
We can all come together as mates.

When will the world be a better place?
Will peoples' apologies be too late?
Imagine the world was a better place.

Anita Rayat (13)
St John's Middle School, Bromsgrove

Imagine The World Was A Better Place

If only there were no more bullies,
That make you feel that you belong in the gullies.

If only there were no more guns,
That make you have unhappy sons.

If only there were no more crimes,
And more people who are known as precious dimes.

If only there were no more fights,
And people pushing you off great heights.

If only there were more people out there,
Who don't just stop and stare.

If only there were no more drugs
And lots more friends to hug.

Amy Hemsley (13)
St John's Middle School, Bromsgrove

159

If Only The World Was A Better Place

If only the world was a better place,
Everyone walked around singing, they were all full of grace.
I think about poverty, war and famine.
Are we really so selfish?
Do we take time to examine?
You see in foreign countries some children don't have rights,
But they're scared to argue or put up a fight.
They just aren't treated equally, it really isn't fair,
Let me ask you something, do you care?
When these suffering children know they might die,
They appreciate everything as time flies by.
Their parents are sad but they've seen it all before,
They can't get the treatment, so they beg for more.
All children should have the right to shelter,
Food and good health,
Because at the end of the day
Keeping the death clock down is more important than wealth.

Erin Henderson (13)
St John's Middle School, Bromsgrove

So Much

So much unsaid that will never be said,
But I hope though my letters will be read,
So much felt that will never be shown again,
But I know the love I gave you will maintain.

So much to see that will never be seen,
But I hope that doesn't kill your spirit to be keen,
So many dreams, I dreamt that will never be real,
Because I made a mistake thinking once a dream
Is real, there's nothing to dream about, but I feel
Different now, I know that some dreams will gleam,
And some will forever stay in their corner shadows,
But you're a living dream, like a sparkling stream.

You flow through many directions drifting away,
From where you started, but your accomplishments
Are from where you were taught how to fly,
Through the many obstacles of life you might face,
So remember life should never be seen as a race.

Don't hold any regrets, because from the worst
Will come something truly through the hardest,
But you'll see something when the sun shines its best,
And things will change, a dream I never knew I had
Will be in you, being you, all grown up and it makes me sad
I won't be there, but I'll know and be glad.

Ruhi-Ur-Rashid (14)
Sidney Stringer Secondary School, Coventry

A Loved One

I think about her all the time,
My heart screams out her gentle name,

But there is no response . . . just silence . . .

I wonder what she is doing every minute of every day,
Hoping she is unharmed,

While I lay on my bed feeling lonely.

I suffer from false illusions,
The way we used to play,
I would chase,
While she would run away.
The way I played with her pearl-white silken soft baby hands,
How her cheeks went bright red as I kissed them,
The way her fragrance embraced the atmosphere,

Blink . . . and there is nothing here.

I used to hold her tightly in my arms and play with her long, straight
Silken, soft brown, hair.

I've lost it all.

It just isn't fair,

I hear and crumble from the sound of her beautiful voice,
Once again I can feel the rejoice.

I get a glimpse at her from a distance (after several months)

The way her face is glowing,
My breath is then taken and I am blown away,

Wishing for her to come back on that special day . . .
We were once two hearts, one soul,
She is the promising piece of my puzzle,
Without the piece I am incomplete,
She is my treasure
And I shall cherish her forever!

Naresh Sahuta (15)
The Bilston High School, Bilston

Life

In life you get one chance,
So don't let it pass with a glance.

Make a difference no matter how small,
And never let your beliefs slip or fall.

Where there's death there's life,
When there's sorrow, there's light.

Always look up, no matter what,
And hold onto what you've got.

Everyone has times when life's hard,
But don't fall back, not even a yard.

On how you make it, life can be great,
So do your best, it's never too late.

Go to school and do your best,
Do all your studying for the test.

Always give out a helping hand
And make sure your life is planned.

Make goals in your life
And soon you will have a lovely wife.

To make sure that you are happy,
Soon you will have to change a nappy.

Nathan Rowton (13)
The Bilston High School, Bilston

My Xbox 360

My Xbox 360 shiny and white,
It cools down through the night.
My Xbox really inspires me
It's better than a Nintendo Wii.
It might be loud but it's still a beaut,
Even when I'm playing 'Call of Duty'.

Joe Adams (12)
The Bilston High School, Bilston

I Cried When I Wrote This

I hope all night you cannot sleep,
And all you do is cry and weep.
For all you did,
I cannot hide,
The reasons why I always lied,
And I hope that when you're sleeping,
Tucked up safe in bed,
All the things you did never left your head.
I heard that when you cry
You never shed a drop,
I pay that when you suffer,
It never ever stops.
I hope that when you scar,
It doesn't heal at least,
I hope that when you bleed,
It will never come to cease.
I hope you burn in Hell,
I hope you drown at sea,
I hope you see the monster
You always were to me.

Alisha Sterling (12)
The Bilston High School, Bilston

Dear Grandad

Today's the day we have to say goodbye,
So you can sail slowly off into the sky.

We love you Grandad with all our heart,
We wish we didn't have to part.

We thank God for taking you only to heal your pain,
That's why we didn't wake you Grandad, what would we gain?

We're glad we weren't there to see you suffer and go,
It only brings regret not to have said goodbye to you
The day you slowly went.

We hope you weren't in pain Grandad,
That's all we have to say,
Except this little message,
We thought of just today.

God please look out for him
For he was one of the best
We hope our darling Grandad
That you are now at rest.

Lisa Marie Davies (14)
The Bilston High School, Bilston

My Mates!

My mates are the best
They are better than the rest
I trust them
With my heart and soul
They are even better than Cheryl Cole
I can tell them secrets
And they would not tell anyone else
Because they trust me
And I trust them
And they are always there for me
When I am lonely
Because they are my one and only.

Sarah Wilkins (12)
The Bilston High School, Bilston

Animal Wonders

Imagine all the animals,
Being let out free,
Imagine all the animals,
Running around with glee.

Dream of all the animals,
Being treated fair,
Dream of all the animals,
Needing good care.

Watch all the animals,
Making all that sound,
Watch all the animals,
Left waiting there to be found.

Think of all the animals,
Waiting there to die,
Think of all the animals,
Already in the sky.

Aleisha Wright (13)
The Grove School, Market Drayton

Let My Wish Run Free

I don't think I should be ashamed
My dream is huge but I can cope
I don't know if it will come true
But all I have to do is hope.

It's a stronger wish that any other dream
This most powerful of dreams
I think of it at night, it pains my kind
It will then force me to scream.

It runs around my head, forever blaring
And I want the world to know
That even though I'm all alone
My dream shall constantly grow.

No hate, no weakness, no war, no crime
Please listen to me
Because if you listen to my wish
You can help to set it free.

The world has been fully enclosed
In everyone's despair
I want a world of blissfulness
And where everything is fair.

Let my voice be heard and overwhelm you
And shock you into silence
And finally you shall stop your hate
And all the war and violence.

I want to create a love
Stronger than love has ever been
And eventually this wish of mine
Can become a real dream.

We can live in fantasy
But only if you listen this time
I shall keep on trying forever and always
With this wonderful dream of mine.

Can you help me let my wish run free?

Emily Fulcher (14)
The Grove School, Market Drayton

Wasting Time - Have A Dream

The time you enjoy wasting,
Is not wasted time.
The time you enjoy spending,
Is always well spent.

If your time balance is negative,
Then take another loan,
For though you may sit all day
On the dock of a bay
You ain't wasting no time.

Its value is high,
Its trust, loyal
My wasted time,
That is,
My unwasted time,
Is the most precious thing I have.

I fly, I can die,
I can fry, I can lie.
I can duck, dodge, do and drown,
All in my wasted time.

I love to waste time,
In my castle on a cloud,
I can't waste time,
On my dock of a bay,
Staring at clouds,
Or even staring at the ceiling.

My world is my time,
My time is my world,
And all in the space of a day,
An hour,
A year,
A minute, second or century.

My dream is this,
For time to be free.
Time to be mine,
To be mine, and everyone's.
Time should be what you want it to be;

Drink, drugs gambling or murder.
Fun, ice creams, sun and sailing.

Be who you want to be,
Be who you are,
Everyone's a hero,
Everyone's a star!

Let time be as you want it
Say and do as you will.
That's what I've done,
And writing this poem's not been a waste of time!

Oliver Hobbs (14)
The Grove School, Market Drayton

Let Mother Nature Rule!

I dream that,
Animals' homes should be restored,
They should roam free,
Let Mother Nature take charge again.

Humans should put right,
All they've done wrong,
Give animals some space,
Let Mother Nature take charge again.

Let the trees grow tall,
The sky be blue,
The grass be green,
Let Mother Nature take charge again.

Humans budge over a bit,
Let the animals have some space,
Give them some freedom,
Let Mother Nature take charge again.

We've ruined this world for long enough,
Let Mother Nature rule again.

Gemma Humphris (14)
The Grove School, Market Drayton

My Dream . . .

Walls are falling
Buildings tumbling
Wars are here
As everybody runs in fear.

This is no dream
A dream is to run and play
No crying or dying
Just a calm, quiet day.

When the bullet hits your head
And it is as fast as a train
Then it suddenly hits your brain
Killing you.

This is no dream
A dream is to run and play
No crying or dying
Just a calm, quiet day.

When the dead man gets stood on
And the blood gets trodden
Then his brains start leaking
Like a waterfall,
And his blood is flooding
Like a tsunami.

This is no dream
A dream is to run and play
No crying or dying
Just a calm, quiet day.

This is my dream
No assassins, no riots
No one gets picked on by their skin colour.

I want the wars to bend
Then I want to look around the bend
And see quiet fields
People getting along
Not saying they look wrong.
Then I can train

To be a footballer
I have a dream
And that's my dream.

Alex Wood (12)
The Grove School, Market Drayton

I Have A Dream

I have a dream,
That you and I can hold hands,
With no judgement around us,
And we can just be friends.

My friend has a dream,
That there was no more pain or wars,
That no more tears were shed or lives lost,
No more flags or countries.

My brother has a dream,
That the water of the world was shared equally,
And hunger and poverty were scarce,
And rich and poor could eat the same food at the same table.

My cousin has a dream,
That skin colour was not judged,
That nobody was ashamed of what they look like,
And everyone was proud of their appearance.

We all have a dream,
That smiles were everywhere and sadness didn't exist,
Those are our dreams,
What are yours?

Rachael Owen (12)
The Grove School, Market Drayton

Just A Teenager

Say you've never met me.
You don't know a thing about me.
You can see me, but not too close up.
You don't know my name, family, upbringing, nothing.
You look at me.
You see one thing:
I'm a teenager.
So it must mean that I drop litter.
I'm a teenager.
So it must mean that I graffiti on park walls.
I'm a teenager.
So it must mean that I lurk about wearing a hood.
I'm a teenager.
So it must mean that I backchat my parents.
I'm a teenager.
So it must mean that I'm an underage drinker.
I'm a teenager.
So it must mean that I 'take over' the children's play area.
I'm a teenager.
So it must mean that I'm inconsiderate.
It must mean that I'm inconsiderate towards the elderly.
It must mean that I'm inconsiderate towards teachers.
It must mean that I'm inconsiderate towards children younger than me.
It must mean that I'm inconsiderate towards the general public.
Towards my own.
Towards my school.
Towards the environment.
Even towards my 'own kind'.

I may be a teenager,
Just a teenager,
But I understand that you're only assuming these things.
Sadly, you're labelling me as a 'typical teenager.'
And I may be just a teenager.
Yet at least I know one thing -

        You were one once.

Lydia Eykelestam (13)
The Grove School, Market Drayton

At Night I Dream, I Pray

Through these tears, I have no regret for my actions
I know you lend me no sympathy
You simply judged all my fears and confusions
I thought you could offer advice or empathy
Tomorrow, I know I will just get snapped at

At night I dream, I pray
I ask the Lord to teach us to have no regrets
For us all to laugh instead of cry so many tears
And for everyone to not hold a grudge, but to forget
I ask for us to move on as the hate clears

You don't know the wounds you have opened
Will heal as scars that shall remain forever
Now all I feel is lonely and abandoned
Crying into my pillow and bed cover
Tomorrow, I know it will happen again

At night I dream, I pray
I dream of a better place
With no violence or hurt
No need to put on a brave face
For people to live happy, instead of buried in dirt

No longer do I want to dream
I want people to see what I've been through
People are not always as they seem
They are normally worse off than you imagine too
Tomorrow, I know as yesterday, I will not matter

At night, I dream, I pray
I wish for people to understand
To love, to know, to feel and to be
I wish everyone was in it together, hand in hand
Wouldn't the world be a nicer place, if everyone could dream like me?

Emma Rich (14)
The Grove School, Market Drayton

A Better Place

I aspire towards ants,
They work as a unit,
A swarm.

They are never alone,
They don't have the capacity,
To argue.

They are treated the same,
There is no leader,
No loser.

A huge monster once broke in,
Attacking the nest with awesome power,
A spider.

The ants swarmed it,
And clung and bit and sometimes
Spat acid.

They hung on even when one of their kin,
Was crushed and killed in the spider's jaws,
Still fighting.

They even adopt other species of ant,
And raise them, despite the obvious differences,
Size and colour.

They are the ultimate species,
Nothing can stand in their way,
Not ever.

And if humans of this Earth work together,
Like ants in a nest, it will make the world,
A better place.

Robert Bosley (14)
The Grove School, Market Drayton

Back To The Beginning . . .

Look beyond the stars,
Into another world,
Let's go back to the beginning,
When couples were lost in love,
Families remained true,
And children had the future engraved in their hearts.

No one judged,
No one stared,
The flowers grew,
The lights passed by
And seconds ticked away.

Trying to fit a square into a circle,
Force a soul to love another
And to turn back time,
Were no lies.

This land of infinite beauty,
Impossible to be destroyed,
So strong,
So perfect,
No need to be disguised.

We didn't need violence to break hearts
Or sadness to forbid dreams,
We didn't need anything,
Anything but belief.

But now it's time to leave
And give back the key,
The key to open this fantasy mind,
The key to be free.

Sophie Peacock (13)
The Grove School, Market Drayton

Dreams

I dream a lot
These dreams shan't stop.
In my head the world is free
In my head there is no violence to see
But when I look
Another dead on the floor
All I can hear
Are screams of fear
All I feel is woe and sorrow
All I hope is there's a different tomorrow

I hope for peace
I hope for cease
Living in a tranquil bubble
No mess, no hurt, no trouble
People walking hand in hand
Everywhere is clean, no pollution on the land
No more fighting
No more war
No hate
Only love
No people in pain on the floor
Fate will give us what we need
Life will be a blooming seed

I have a dream
This has been seen
I have a dream
But until this war is over
This dream cannot come true.

Ellesse Dee Wilson (14)
The Grove School, Market Drayton

I Have A Dream

This is my dream, this is my need
This is my dream, I have a dream.

No more hate - no more heartache
This is my dream I don't want it to break.
Everyone's laughing under the sun
Everyone's having fun.

This is my dream. This is my need
This is my dream
I have a dream

All the air is clean,
There isn't a dirty stream!
All the animals are roaming free.
Not one of them in captivity!
Everywhere's music, everywhere's laughter
We still feel the same after.

This is my dream. This is my need
This is my dream I have a dream.

Aid helps our band, no pollution on our land.
No rich, no poor,
Nor civil war!
This is my dream, this is my need.
This is my dream. I have a dream.

Love is from the heart!
It's a brand new start.
Keep the love in your heart!

Abbie Hickson (11)
The Grove School, Market Drayton

I Have A Vision Of Freedom

I have a vision,
That vision is that there is freedom everywhere,
That there is freedom in the plants,
Freedom in the animals,
Freedom in the world
Freedom in ourselves,
Freedom out of our cultures.

A vision that this freedom is pure,
That this freedom is not for one,
That this freedom is for all.

A vision to show what freedom is,
Freedom is not what you think,
Freedom is not what anybody thinks,
I wouldn't have a vision of it if it was already there,
Would I?
That's why.

I have a vision,
A vision to prove that a free society is a place where it is safe
                                                    to be unpopular,
To prove that to have a vision without action is a daydreamer;
And that action without vision is a nightmare,
I have a vision that will have action,
Therefore this vision will come true,
One day,
And I will prove to you then,
I had a vision.

Paul Hammond (14)
The Grove School, Market Drayton

178

Can You See It?

A world without weapons
Can you see it?
A world without discrimination
Can you see it?
A world without segregation
Can you see it?
A world where no one is left out
Can you see it?
A world where gang violence is a myth
Can you see it?
A world where we only see the positive
Can you see it?
A world where backgrounds don't matter
Can you see it?
A world where wars are extinct
Can you see it?
A world where poverty is banished
Can you see it?
A world where you can achieve anything
Can you see it?
A world where you can be free to live your life
Can you see it?
A world where we are in control of our future
Can you see it?
A world where we unite as one
I can see it
Can you?

Angela Penfold (14)
The Grove School, Market Drayton

Want A Friend, Be A Friend

I'm scared
All alone
No love
No home.

Wishing that
I could find
Someone to care
Someone who's kind.

Tail drooped,
Whimpering cries
Will anyone notice my
Welling eyes?

I followed their rule
But I did one bark
They shouted and hit
As I was thrown into the dark.

My life is coming
To an end
I need someone
To be my friend.

Then I saw a kind face
That was how I was found
She took me to a loving place
Where love does make the world go round.

Jasmine Humphrey (13)
The Grove School, Market Drayton

Change

The world is changing
All the time
But is all of this change good?

People are more accepting
Different races stand together as one
Although there are still exeptions
At least some of the hate is gone

But still the wars are raging on
There are more and more weapons every day
People full of anger, but why?
The happiness is clouded by grey

The world is becoming more equal
Gender and race means less and less
Equality's growing, all through the world
Trying to make sense of our mess

But abuse, too, is growing more
From a father to child, a mother to baby
People crying and dying but nobody cares
It's getting out of hand and it's crazy

So is all this change a good thing or bad?
Is the world getting better or worse?
Are we feeling the love, or being filled with hate?
Is this change a blessing or curse?

Allison Smith (14)
The Grove School, Market Drayton

Change

We need change
I dream of a world where black equals white
And we could live with each other without hatred or spite
I dream of a land where hatred is banished
Racism, bullying and stereotypes have vanished
Leaders of the world can meet together
Respecting each other, making promises that last forever
Don't take their word for it, it's lies, all lies
One day they make peace with each other
The next thousands die
Why?
Why do we live in a world where no soul is equal?
A world where in one country a man gets paid less in a year
Than a man in another gets paid in a day?
A world where straight is greater than gay?
These are the questions that I ask
Why do these so-called 'leaders and 'peace makers' let it all happen?
Murderers, rapists, racists walk the streets with a smug grin
They affect one life along with its kin
All of these are terrible things but they are all real
The only way we can stop it is if we all stand together
Don't wait for people to do it, get out there and do it
Leaders of the world
People of the world
We need change!

Bradlee Webb (13)
The Grove School, Market Drayton

What If . . .

What if we could start again
A new planet, a new land, a new home
And everything is perfect and happy
Enough food, enough water, enough love?
What if we don't take advantage of our land
And just live a natural life that we should?

What if the plants and animals were free,
Able to do what they want, and be equal to Man?
They have their own mind, own ideas, own life
No need to kill and hunt for them
They are equal, they are free.

What if all the things never run dry?
No climate change, no disasters, no threats
The objects are unlimited, and reusable too
The things will never die out.

What if there was no unpredictability?
No need to be worried, sad or upset?
Everything is set in stone, no sudden sadness.

What if we could live forever
No illness, no sickness, no pain?

What if . . .?

Matthew Orgill (14)
The Grove School, Market Drayton

Today Without Tomorrow

People without pain,
School kids without shame.
Fright without fear,
Nightfall without near.
Stars without skies,
Hellos without his.
Fire without flame,
Gambling without gain.
Hatred without heat,
Flying without fleet.
Pace without pitch,
Gameplay without glitch.
Finish without fault,
Humming without halt.
Talk without terror,
Edit without error.

Stacey Muir (14)
The Grove School, Market Drayton

A Dreaming Forest

Silver slicken beams slipped through wily branches
Dreaming dreamily dreams drifted on a drifting wind
Hazy thoughts were mixed into a whirlwind of idea
Dark smooth shadows met lightbeams of the barren moon
Voices and thoughts echoed throughout the dreamy forest
Passing people passed through seemingly portalled woods
Rustling rusty-coloured oak leaves rustled
The rippling crispy dry leaves crunched underneath foot
Veiny veined eyes dazzled by beaming beams

A new beaming light of lunar rays and daylight rays shone
Giving graceful rainbow rays of hope
Shining into every shadow of dark and beam of light
Bringing alive hope for a peaceful dreaming forest.

Joseph Wilcock (14)
The Grove School, Market Drayton

The Valley

Have you ever been to The Valley?
I have.
Once you're there, you won't be able to leave.
It won't let you.
The Valley longs for the odd visitor, or the lost traveller.
It thrives on your fear, your thirst to escape.
It very much draws you in, all the many
Plants and wildlife.
I fell for the trick.
I unknowingly approached the area.
Suddenly, shadows engulf the Valley, as if
All the happiness wearily disappears into nothing.
All the plants die, the animals flee.
And then . . .
Darkness!

Kyle Edwards (13)
The Grove School, Market Drayton

I Dream Of . . .

I dream of a place that bears no hate
Where love is served upon a golden plate.

I dream of a world where there is
No war
A world where no one will want more

I dream of a paradise where bullying is a thing of the past
Everyone respecting the flag on the mast

I dream of a Heaven upon this Earth
Where everyone's equal and has
Got no worth

I have a dream of a planet with no racists
Everyone's view is respected even
If you're an atheist.

Will Potts (14)
The Grove School, Market Drayton

185

I Wish . . .

I wish that I could reach the moon,
And hold it hand in hand.
I wish that I could touch the stars,
And never reach the land.

I wish that I can sail the seas,
And never reach the port.
I wish I could stop racism,
Isn't that a thought?

I wish that I could stop drugs,
And everyone be free.
I wish that I can see the world,
For all it used to be.
I wish that I can live forever,
In this happy memory.

Brogan Ashley (12)
The Grove School, Market Drayton

A Revolution

A revolution
No more repeating history,
It's time to change.
Give black and white equal rights.

A revolution
No more repeating history,
It''s time to think.
No more tsunamis, peace within our armies.

A revolution
No more repeating history,
It's time to change.
A life ending in pain is a life given in vain.

A revolution.

Alice Booker (14)
The Grove School, Market Drayton

Why?

I dream of a world with no war
Every country getting along
No nuclear weapons
No killing the innocent.

I dream of a world with no bullying
There's no need for it
So why do it?

I dream of a world without racism
Every colour and race getting along.

This would create a near perfect world
So why do these things keep on happening?
Why?

Grant Freail (14)
The Grove School, Market Drayton

Why?

Why?
All alone on the cold streets of Leeds,
Kicked out because I didn't look right,
A loud voice,
A hard smack on my bony back,
Shivering in the rain,
Hiding between the dustbins,
Groans from my hungry stomach,
Searching for a tiny morsel of food,
Finally I find a half-eaten takeaway,
A pile of cardboard boxes is my bed for tonight,
What's going to happen tomorrow?
What did I do wrong?

Zoe Worthington (14)
The Grove School, Market Drayton

Chloe's Fantasy

Welcome to Chloe's Fantasy,
A vision of how the world should be.
No hate, no war, no discrimination
And she's hoping it would spread throughout the nation . . .

She has this amazing dream,
Where everyone comes together as a team.
We'd work together,
As we should forever.

Nothing is counted by the colour of your skin,
And everyone would not sin.
This is Chloe's Fantasy,
A vision of how the world should be.

Chloe Bentley (14)
The Grove School, Market Drayton

I Have A Dream

I have a dream that the world one day
Will be a better place.
That all the people on this Earth,
Will be a happy race.

The fighting and killing, abuse and terror,
Will forever cease.
And then this life of ours,
Will be a life of peace.

So I hope this dream of mine,
Will hopefully come true.
And the pleasures that this life will bring,
Means happiness for me and you.

Cameron Matthews (11)
The Grove School, Market Drayton

Together We Shall Stand

Together we shall stand,
Together we shall stand wherever and forever.

Together we shall rise,
Together we shall rise with power
At every hour.

Today we shall unite
Throughout day and night.

This is where we shall stand,
Together we are one.

Jordan Domagalski (14)
The Grove School, Market Drayton

Rise

Rise for power
Upon this dark hour
Rise for salvation
As a nation
Rise for health
And all its wealth
Rise for peace
Let hatred cease
Rise for a dream
With your team.

Harry DuBois-Jones (13)
The Grove School, Market Drayton

Stand As One

Racism comes in many shapes and forms,
Sadly, most people have had their fair share since they were born,
Judged before they have even been given a chance,
Slowing down their future for their career to advance.

Why can't people say we're all the same?
Standing next to each other, this isn't a game,
Let's be at peace, each of us standing hand in hand,
Let's all be with one another and make a stand.

Clayton Ashley (14)
The Grove School, Market Drayton

Superstar!

Superstar in the sky,
With wings so I can fly so high.
Shows all day,
Pose all night,
Limousines - what a sight!
Mansions galore,
With all I adore,
Curly hair,
Work what's there,
No one moans,
Because everyone knows I'm a superstar!
I guess for now,
But I don't know how,
Stardom will have to hold,
Whilst I'm growing old,
All my ambitions,
Are for a future mission.
So when you look
At the TV,
Think of me for 1, 2, 3.
I have a dream that some day I will be a superstar.

Lisa Appleby (13)
The High Arcal School, Dudley

A Soldier's Dream

If I could change the world,
I would banish violence and war,
Destruction would be no more.

No wish is too small,
No wish is too big.

War is brutal,
War is savage,
Soldiers aren't heroes.

No wish is too small,
No wish is too big.

This is why I am ashamed,
Ashamed of myself knowing,
Soldiers aren't heroes.

No wish is too small,
No wish is too big.

In the desolate war-scarred streets of Iraq,
I stand dejected,
Waiting for attack.

No wish is too small,
No wish is too big.

The thick musky air tickles my senses,
Clogging my throat,
Blocking my nose.

No wish is too small,
No wish is too big.

My heart is pounding,
I could be next,
I could be dead.

No wish is too small,
No wish is too big.

Hannah Winfield (13)
The High Arcal School, Dudley

Lets . . .

War is a murderous thing
Let's try and stop this happening
Is it just so you can become a king?
Let's try and stop this happening
Boys become men
Let's try and stop this happening
They have to start talking, using a ballpoint pen
Let's try and stop this happening
They go to the bloodshed battle
Let's try and stop this happening
Instead of helping you feed the cattle
Let's try and stop this happening
Innocent people dying
Let's try and stop this happening
The last thing they do is cry
Let's try and stop this happening
I hope one day
Let's start making this dream happen
That soon at the end of May
Let's start making this dream happen
I won't need to fear
Let's start making this dream happen
That every time, in the car, when my mum turns a gear
Let's start making this dream happen
That someone is shot down
Let's start making this dream happen
That people that frown
Let's start making this dream happen
Will be able to turn it the other way round
Let's start making this dream happen
Because there will be no more . . .
Let's start making this dream happen
War, war, war!

Caitlin Stewart (13)
The High Arcal School, Dudley

Why Won't It Stop?

Hi, my name is Mary,
And I look quite hairy,
I get bullied a lot,
By a boy called Harry Scott.
Why won't it stop?

He calls me names,
And plays his games,
I don't find them funny,
But he still takes my money.
Why won't it stop?

He hit me once and
Called me a 'dunce',
I collapsed and said
'I wish I was dead!'
Why won't it stop?

It's not just at school, it's at home too!
When I am naughty, Mommy hits me with a shoe,
I haven't got a daddy,
Because Mommy thought he was a baddie!
Why won't it stop?

Mommy doesn't see,
What she does to me,
She needs help,
Otherwise I'm going to yelp!
Why won't it stop?

Harry Scott stopped bullying me,
After the teacher saw what he was doing to everybody,
Mommy stopped hitting me too,
After getting some help from a woman called Sue!
It did stop and now I love my life!

Sian Halford (13)
The High Arcal School, Dudley

Freedom

I have a dream of the best world of all,
Where everybody lives as an equal,
Never put down for their skin or clothes,
If only that was the way it now goes.

I have a dream that no one was cruel,
That there was never a brutal duel,
We all get on with the others around,
Never making a sound.

I have a dream that some weren't alive,
But that ruins my vision for all to thrive,
All I want is some respect for others,
Why should smart ones be the victims of 'bruvas?

I have a dream that none were shied away,
And none were intimidated by what others would say,
We all have a voice inside, screaming out loud,
That's one of the reasons that we should feel proud.

I have a dream that we all were green,
This dream beholds the best world ever seen,
Let's make ourselves the ozone's protection,
Finally at peace from worries of pollution.

I have a dream that no one was sad,
That nobody was evil, mean or bad,
If we all worked together we'd give an amazing life,
Never at worry from death from a knife.

I have a dream that my dream would come true,
A better life for all, even me and you,
I want all to hear my voice in the crowd,
If only I wasn't a cowardly coward.

Oh, what a world.

Tom Shaw (13)
The High Arcal School, Dudley

I Have A Dream

I have a dream, where the grass is green,
And is short and never-ending.
Where the trees form a city with its untamed branches
Of hope and faith.
Where the flowers shoot out of the ground, smiling in the sun
As they grow
That is my dream.

I have a dream where the rubbish bins are never left starving.
Where the waste tips are no longer standing
And their old belongings make new everyday items.
That is my dream.

I have a dream where we make our fortunes come true,
Get good opportunities and job offers.
Where we have the money we need and no recession to spoil it.
Where good honest people make a good honest living while working
With one another.
Where people do not worry about losing their jobs
And there is no need for benefits.
That is my dream.

I have a dream, where people live in their own countries
Without fear of war. Of violence. Of terrorism. Of death.
Where people have never heard of poverty and AIDs.
Where people get on with one another and do not have petty arguments.
That is my dream.

There is a dream, where armies exist!
Where we send boys to their deaths
Where bombs land and guns fire
And where soldiers die!
In Iraq 179 soldiers died and in Afghanistan 150 also died.
This is not my dream.

Daniel Southall (13)
The High Arcal School, Dudley

The Dream

I have a dream
To change the world
For man, woman, boy and girl
To rid of all that stresses us
To banish the pain from all of us

You have a dream?
To banish recession
As money problems cause depression
Those children will no longer be destitute
And those greedy fat cats' money will be given the boot.

And in this dream there will also be
No pollution caused by you or me
No waste, no rubbish at our feet
Just ground and clear, just clear streets.

I have a dream
For those sorrowful souls
To have their much needed love, and ignite their bones
Orphans will have real life, real food, real homes
No longer will they be slaved or hurt or cold

Another dream
It'd be nice to say
There's no bad future coming our way
No starvation, no disease, no viral plague
You live a full life and a late dying age.

Oh this dream this dream
My dream, my dream
I want this as truth, reality
Help me make this dream become real life
I have a dream, it can come alive.

Laura Horton (12)
The High Arcal School, Dudley

I Have A Dream!

I have a dream
That the world will be at peace
Having a day that's just a feast
I have a dream
That the world will be a better place
With a smile drawing on everyone's face.
I have a dream
Where no one gets hurt
And everyone is in one piece
I have a dream
Where there won't be a fight
Where everything is plain white
I have a dream
Where the world is full of flowers
Instead of the human ashes
I have a dream
That nothing gets broken
So the love will be a token.

Imagine the world at peace
Everyone's emotions are happy, at peace.

Don't let the dream go away
Keep it with you through the rough times

If words change the world,
Then what will emotions change?

Don't imagine the dream going
I dream,
I dream,
I dream.

Megan Chapman (13)
The High Arcal School, Dudley

To Let . . .

Let,
Everyone be free.
Let,
Everyone be treated equally.
Let,
White be friends with black.
Let,
People know they're all the same.
Let,
The nation know we all have the same heart.
Let,
Black in the same room.
Let,
People do as they please.
Let,
White know we feel locked up.
Let's,
Show we are not scared to leave the house.
Let,
Black children live a life.
Let,
Us tell you we feel upset and alone.
Let,
Everyone be happy.
Let,
Us thank you
Because we are all on the same Earth
And have the right to be free.

Chloe James (13)
The High Arcal School, Dudley

I Want A New Daddy!

My name is Caddy,
I'm abused by my daddy
I wish it would stop,
Before I pop.
Why me?

I got hit with Baby Tommy,
When all I wanted was my mommy,
She will never come back,
After Daddy broke her back,
Why me?

Baby Tommy gets hit as well,
But daddy would kill me if I ever tell,
It's not just physical, it's verbal too,
I wish I had a daddy who would do what he was meant to do!
Why me?

Now I live with my new mommy and daddy,
Along with my new sister, Maddy.
Daddy is at home,
All alone with no one to hurt or abuse.
Poor him!

Daddy had to spend seven years in prison,
But I'm glad because me and Tommy live a better life,
Every day I'm allowed out to play
And every time I say . . .
Lucky me!

Emily Ash (13)
The High Arcal School, Dudley

I Have A Dream!

Imagine a world with no crime,
No justice, no prison, not even a tear,
It causes great pain and an action you will regret,
Not even a day that would go by in a prison cell,
That you would sit alone and fear for what becomes.

Crime, a violent and regretful action,
That at the time is cool,
A body lying in the dark, food taken from a shop,
Many gangs of prejudice, but who to stop this becoming.
Is this really so cool?

Imagine a world with no crime,
No justice, no prison, not even a tear,
It causes great pain and an action you will soon regret,
Not even a day that would go by in a prison cell
That you would sit alone and fear for what becomes.

Crime, a violent and regretful action,
That creates no peace but justice,
What if there were no police,
Or even guards to stop this?
What will become of the world?

You, only you can change such crime only if you wish,
Sit alone and think, if you don't change, what will?
Crime could get worse, when nothing's left or nobody around to murder.
What will happen then?
Imagine a world with no crime!

Bethany Edwards (13)
The High Arcal School, Dudley

Bullying

They really must have no idea,
How this makes me feel,
Being on my own all day,
Living with this fear.

Please, please tell me what have I done?
Do I deserve this pain and misery?
I feel so wrong,
All I wanna do is run.

Sitting down, eating my lunch,
I'm shadowed over,
My corner becomes dark,
I fear you will punch.

You throw me sharply to the ground,
'Give me your money, you sad geek!'
I empty my pockets,
I don't make a murmur, I don't make a sound.

This is what our world has come to,
All over the world,
Black, white or yellow,
It could happen to you.

Couldn't all the hating drop?
More loving,
More loving,
So all the bullying will stop.

Lauren Jeavons (13)
The High Arcal School, Dudley

You

You walk into the classroom
See me sitting alone,
All wrapped up,
In a world of my own.

I'm thinking that thought,
I'm dreaming that dream,
Of what my life will be like,
When we're twenty-three.

I'll be living in London,
I'll be working with stars,
It's a dream out of reach,
Yet so close to my heart.

The wars will be over
People will be treated the same,
But that world's not this one,
But you help me keep sane.

You always listen to me,
While I'm going on and on,
You make me feel special,
When you're the special one.

What's the inspiration?
What makes this dream true?
The answer is simple,
The inspiration is you.

Sami Shaw (13)
The High Arcal School, Dudley

I Had A Dream Last Night . . .

I had a dream last night
Where the world was not at war
Every country got along
And never wanted more!

I had a dream last night
Where the people were united
Colours, religions and even supporters
Of Manchester United!

I had a dream last night
Where the murders would just freeze
Innocent people were not dying
Don't let me wake up, please!

I had a dream last night
Where there was no suffering
A thing called death was not ending their pain
And perfect people were never suffering.

I had a dream last night
Where all bad people were banished
Unfortunately, when I woke up
I realised my dreams had vanished!

Dreaming is not for people
Who always have a moan
Dreaming is for people who will help
Unravel the new world we can own . . . *together.*

Katie Smith (13)
The High Arcal School, Dudley

The World Will See

I wake up in the morning
To be greeted by my cat
His lovely little face
As he sits upon the mat
But how badly was he treated
By the family he once knew?
Fed acid, dumped and nearly killed
By the cruelty of the few.

Then I wander to the kitchen
Past my dog sat by the wall
With her lovely eyes all shiny
And her paws wrapped round her ball
But again she was a victim
Of the family from Hell
Beaten, starved and treated bad
But now she is doing well.

I will never understand them
How they treated them so bad
Why they were cruelly harmed
And made so very sad
But the lovely little creatures
My friends will always be
And I hope this is a lesson
That the world will always see.

Laura Jones (13)
The High Arcal School, Dudley

I Have A Dream

I have a dream,
A glimpse of hope,
A wish to help people
And save their souls

To end the blood and murder
Of innocent people,
Families taken away;
Remains blown to bits

I talk of course, of a dream to end . . .
Wars and murder,
Pity young lads,
Instantly aged into soldiers
Who dream of glory but face despair.

Once babies and toddlers, carefree, cherished.
Now cradle and dust,
Never again will they feel
The love and fuss of family.

What feeds this Devil?
It may be religion,
It might be politics,
But do these innocent children
Deserve death because of it?

Emma Jones (13)
The High Arcal School, Dudley

Go Back, Go Forward Children I See

My friend is Claire,
She got hit with a chair,
Her body is covered in bruises,
It's not the life she chooses

Go back, go forward
Children I see.

The family for her,
Is calm with a chauffeur,
Claire's mom is very violent,
But Claire just stays silent.

Go back, go forward
Children I see.

Her life would be better,
If she just got her mom a helper,
No food she eats,
Until she weeps.

Go back, go forward
Children I see.

I am her only friend
Why?
Because this nightmare has no end.

Amie Malpass (13)
The High Arcal School, Dudley

I Have A Dream

I have a dream that one day there will be no racism in the world,
That all the children in the world dying of diseases
Get treated, taken care of, given a home and are loved.

Why should people be judged by the colour of their skin?
At the end of the day we are all human,
Do you want to die lonely because you took racism too far?

I have a dream that homeless people are taken off the streets
That they are taken care of and fed,
Out the cold and that they are helped to find a job
To live their life once more.

Money is printed new every day
So why isn't that money used to make new homes for homeless people,
And the children dying in Africa?

The Government say they have no money
But we all know that in factories all over the world
There is money being printed
That could be used for something good.

So I have a dream that one day
People will feel loved and happy,
People will not be homeless
And we will start to care once more!

Georgina Salt (13)
The High Arcal School, Dudley

I have A Dream To Be Lady Gaga

In my sparkly gown all I can hear is the screams of the crowd.
I can faintly see them through the black tinted windows
Of my personal pink limousine.
The limo comes to a smooth stop and my chauffeur
Swiftly opens the door.
I place one leg out of the door as I place my huge
Gucci sunglasses on.
I strut onto the famous red carpet and strike my stunning pose.
At the same time I am blinded by the pap's camera flashbulbs.
Suddenly autograph books come flying at me
Like hungry eagles as the pens follow.
But there is only time to sign a few.
Send the signed books back flying
And I blow a precious kiss to my fans.
When I finally arrive inside I soon realise that there is no time
To sit down as my name is already being called out for a nomination.
Then before I know it I am the winner of Best Female Artist.
I strut down the gold stairs flicking my blonde full fringe.
I get to the stage as I cannot believe my luck
That I have won an award at the Brit Awards.
I pick up my award it all comes crashing down.
I open my eyes and realise I was dreaming.
Am I really Lady Gaga? Nah, I wish!

Charlotte Regen (13)
The High Arcal School, Dudley

I Have A Dream

Imagine a world without war
It's like a world without death
Soldiers go out just to be killed
You do something, take a breath.

Your family and friends probably died
Out on a field with savage guns
They drop down into bloodbaths
Then they make orphan sons.

This is because of us and our Prime Minister
Accusing countries of a crime
The Prime Minister's son doesn't go out
They stand at the back of the line.

Every day there is a war
Between squabbling towns
We should live in a world of peace
And not act like stupid clowns.

So, you do something and save our country
From evil Bin Laden wannabes
Why go to war for one person
When you could lock him up so he's stuck like the trees?
Imagine a world without war.

Jake Longshaw (13)
The High Arcal School, Dudley

Dear Diary

Dear Diary,
Cowered in the corner, curled in a ball,
Whimpering in fear, the result of a brawl,
I have done nothing apart from be smart,
I have a dream, oh where do I start?

Dear Diary,
I never signed up for this life,
Shaking, scared of fear from the knife,
I see them approach and my heart starts to beat,
I feel terrified so much, from head to my feet.

Dear Diary,
A slash of my wrists,
A punch from their fists,
A bruise in my eye,
Until next time, it's goodbye.

Dear Diary,
I have a dream, oh where do I start?
Just to pick up the pieces of my shattered heart,
Maybe one day they will leave me at peace,
If only all the bullying would finally cease.

Signed, Victim.

Alex Richards (13)
The High Arcal School, Dudley

My Dream

Imagine if we all achieve our own dreams,
We live the way we want,
Nobody there to stop you
That is my dream.

I have a dream of walking through that tunnel,
To hear all the screams of your own fans,
To have that feeling inside you,
That is my dream.

I have a dream of playing on that court,
With all those different weathers,
Against all those different people,
That is my dream

I have a dream playing on different courts,
In different countries,
On my own private jet,
That is my dream.

I have a dream of playing against Nadal,
In the final of Wimbledon,
Beating him in straight sets,
That is my dream.

Adam Dorsett (12)
The High Arcal School, Dudley

Pick On Me

You can pick on me if you want,
I might be too fat, or too ugly,
But does that give you the right
To bully?

You can call me names,
But it doesn't give you power,
It doesn't give you the authority
To bully.

You can make me sad,
You can make me cry,
But does it make you feel big,
When you bully?

You might feel impressed,
You might even feel proud,
But just think
How does the other person feel?

Think about your actions,
Think about the consequences,
Think about the meaning of happiness
And think does a bully have it?

Jenny Littler (13)
The High Arcal School, Dudley

212

I Believe

I believe that black people and white people will work together
And join as one.
I believe together we are strong as brothers and sisters.
Let's share this world.
No longer will black people be treated different.
We will have world peace and nothing can change that.
I believe we will get unity not war
We are all equal.
Freedom does exist.
We will forgive and forget.
I believe that we are all equal.
We will walk down the streets together.
Show racism the red card.
Love is coming down to Earth.
We may be facing war.
Put down your weapons because we are as one.
I believe we cannot walk alone
And as we walk we must make the pledge
That as we march forward in life
We will not turn back
We walk as unity, I believe.

Scott Melville (13)
The High Arcal School, Dudley

My Perfect World

I'd like to live in a world
Where people are free from disease
That kills no one, not you, not me.

I'd like to live in a world
Where we are safe to walk the streets
Without being stabbed or beat.

I'd like to live in a world
Free from war
Where young boys would die no more.

I'd like to live in a world
Where money means nothing
But, we value family as everything.

I'd like to live in a world
Free from murder, no crime, no evil
A perfect Utopia.

I hope this does come true
For me, for you
A perfect life, no trouble, no strife.

Ethan Penson (13)
The High Arcal School, Dudley

I Have A Dream

I have a dream that there will be food on every table,
Every plate and every country.
War will be stopped in every village,
Every hour and every place.
People will live in harmony with each other.
No one will be alone, the will would be united as one.

There will be a home for the homeless,
No matter who or where they are.
The parents will be there to spend the special time with their family.

Ben Emery (13)
The High Arcal School, Dudley

My Poem

I have a dream
That black and white people will hold hands
I have a dream
That the world is bad
I have a dream
We will fight till the end
I have a dream
That we will win the fight
I have a dream
That we will be free
I have a dream
That racial harmony will soon come
I have a dream
That justice will be ours
I have a dream
That freedom is here
I have a dream
That we are free at last
I have a dream
Peace at last!

Ryan Cross (12)
The High Arcal School, Dudley

I Have A Dream

I have a dream that violence will stop and that peace will be made.
What have the other countries done to us
To make us cause all this pain and suffering,
And all the heartache to all the families of the lives we have taken?
Can't we just get along instead of the suffering we cause?
Why don't we minus the violence and increase the peace?
Make the world a better and peaceful place
By stopping the fighting, violence and war between the countries

That is my dream.

Savanah Ram (13)
The High Arcal School, Dudley

Just Think

Just think
Do you have a dream?
Just think
What that dream can do.
Just think
Will this nation rise?
Just think
Can everyone be treated the same?
Just think
Can you forgive?
Just think
Can you forget?
Just think
This is our hope.
Just think
This is our faith.
Just think
We cannot walk alone.
Just think
We cannot turn back.

Gemma Harding & Molly Lawley (12)
The High Arcal School, Dudley

Just Imagine . . .

Imagine a world where we have peace at last
Where children play in the street, and do not vanish,
Where there is no fear or despair for the elderly,
Where people come together and unite
Imagine . . .

Imagine a world with a smile engraved on the surface of the Earth
With people's hearts filled with love instead of hatred.
With no blood baths or defeats,
Just imagine . . .

Imagine a world who can give people a second chance,
Who can make the illness and deaths disappear
Who can make us live forever in peace with each other
Just imagine . . . imagine.

Imagine a world that can look down on us
And see no blood covering the ground like a bonnet
And see no pain and hurt in people's eyes,
But only see hope and happiness for the future.
Just imagine, imagine, imagine . . .

Johanna Whettall (13)
The High Arcal School, Dudley

It Takes Just One

There's nowhere I can go,
Without feeling low.

Even though I'm dreaming,
I can't block out my own screaming.

Even though my heart is beating inside
I feel like it's going down an empty slide.

I finally get to the end,
Suddenly, swerve a bend.

I'm back into the world,
Full of nightmare and things that leer,
It's time to face up to my own fear.

I try to get through, showing no fear,
I feel like I'm nothing and no none can hear.

It takes just one to stand up and be brave,
Even thought they don't realise how
Many they can save.

Rebekah Jones (13)
The High Arcal School, Dudley

I Have A Dream To Dance!

I have a dream, a dream
To dance, to perform, to sing
I want to choreograph stars of the future
I want to be *big!*

I have a dream, a dream
To meet new people, to make deals, to sign contracts
I want to feel my adrenaline rush
I want to be *big!*

I have a dream, a dream
To thrive, to feel excited, to hear people scream my name,
I want to help other people find fame
I want to be *big!*

I have a dream, a dream
To see my name in lights, to see my dances
On stages like the West End
I want to be b*ig!*
I want to dance, entrance, enthral, mesmerise!

Nikki McFarlane (12)
The High Arcal School, Dudley

Black And White

Why can't
Everyone be free?
Why can't
Racism stop?
Why can't
People stop being judged
Why can't
We face our feelings, care?
Why can't
People be judged by character?
Why can't
We all stick together?
Why can't
We believe in people in different races, together.
Why can't
We all be the same race?
Why can't
People forgive and forget it?

Heidi Singh (12)
The High Arcal School, Dudley

My Poem

You must believe!
We will fight till the end
Hallelujah
We are equally the same
Hallelujah
This is not the end, but a beginning
Hallelujah
Our dreams will come true
Hallelujah
Racial harmony will be here
Hallelujah
We will walk together, not alone
Hallelujah
Freedom will be ours
Hallelujah
Peace at last! Peace at last!
Hallelujah
Free.

Harry Street (13)
The High Arcal School, Dudley

I Dream

I dream that one day we will be all equal,
That white and black people will be able to sit on the bus together
Shake hands together.

Yes we all dream but I dream so much that it's almost real.
I dream that my children will not be racist,
And that one day they will live in harmony with people
And that, not just that, you are equal
And it's not about the colour of your skin.
It's about who you are.
So why can't that perfect world be today?
Because if you don't know love, you don't know life!

I dream that me and you are fair
We are all equal, white people are not doormats for this country
                                                    or any other,

It's not about hate
Black people are like any other
So I say just see past the colour of people's skin.

Sophie Faulkner (12)
The High Arcal School, Dudley

I Have A Dream

I have a dream that one day there will be no selfishness and greed,
That everyone will have what they need,
There will be no more poverty, selfishness and greed.

I would love to live in a world where money is no more,
You wouldn't have to buy anything.
Everyone would have enough,
You could explore life to its full.

Imagine a world with no suffering,
No sadness or misery,
Every moment is full of joy,
Everyone is kind to each other.

James Cash (13)
The High Arcal School, Dudley

Our World

Our world is full of violence,
Our world is full of tears,
Our world is full of hatred,
Our world is full of fears.

Our world should have no violence,
Our world should always care,
No matter what the colour,
No matter who or where.

Our world is full of poverty,
Our world is full of dread,
Our world is full of prejudice,
Suffering and bloodshed.

Our world should have no poverty,
With all races combined,
Our world should be healthy,
I care because it's mine.

Hannah Shaw (12)
The High Arcal School, Dudley

A Dream . . .

A dream that one day black and white people will be treated the same.
A dream that black and white people can sit together on the bus.
A dream that there will be peace in the world.
A dream that black and white people can walk down the same
street together.
A dream that people would be judged for their character
Of the person, not the colour of their skin
A dream that one day the world will be in harmony!
A dream where the world was a family.
A dream where celebrations were celebrated together!

Where is the love?

Vicky Marston (13)
The High Arcal School, Dudley

I Had A Dream!

I had a dream that black and white people were equal.
I had a dream black and white people were allowed
                                on the same bus together.
I had a dream black and white people were allowed to live in the
                                same street in harmony.
Where is the love?
I had a dream there was peace in the world.
I had a dream people were not judged by the colour of their skin
I had a dream celebrations should be celebrated together.
I had a dream that the world was a family.
Where is the love?
I had a dream that nobody disobeyed others.
I had a dream you must believe that black and white people were
                                treated the same.

That one day the world would change.
Where is the love?
Can it all end in a good way?

Chloe Lloyd (12)
The High Arcal School, Dudley

I Wish, I Wish

I cannot walk home alone without feeling scared,
I wish, I wish I could change this,
Turning a corner gives me a scare,
I wish, I wish I could change this,
Graffiti makes our world become scruffy,
I wish, I wish I could change this,
Child abuse is really cruel,
I wish, I wish I could change this,
Racism harms us all,
I wish, I wish I could change this.

But why is our world like this?
I have a dream one day we can change this.

Danielle Richards (13)
The High Arcal School, Dudley

224

Racism – Haikus

Racism is wrong,
Skin colour has affected,
Some views all along.

Race shouldn't matter,
Looks change views at the first glance,
Like thin or fatter.

Don't care black or white,
Wars about culture happen,
Race shouldn't cause fights.

Jews died - World War II
Opposing religions fight,
For what? No one knew.

Racism why? Why?
There is no reason for it,
People hurt and dead.

Ellen Bishop (13)
The High Arcal School, Dudley

Dream World

Imagine a world without pollution
Imagine a world without crime
Imagine a world without all the fighting
I wish that world would be mine.

Imagine a world without greedy people
Imagine a world without stress
Imagine a world without money problem
So I could go buy a new dress.

I wish that this world was so real
I wish that this dream would come true
I wish that our world could be better
Oh, isn't my dream your dream too?

Jade Walker (13)
The High Arcal School, Dudley

Imagine A World

Imagine no war, no crime
Imagine happiness and relief
Imagine no more murders or fights
Streets no longer scary at night.

Families of soldiers in worry and dread
Not knowing if loved ones are buried and dead
Innocent people not safe on the street
Unaware of the people they'll meet.

Knives and guns are what they take
To use on people they apparently 'hate'
A world that's a war zone
But was it always this bad?

Imagine a place happy and safe
Imagine a world with no more anger and hate . . .

Ellie Parton (13)
The High Arcal School, Dudley

I Have A Dream

I have a dream,
That black and white people will unite.

I have a dream,
That no one else will be racist.

I have a dream,
That there will be no more discrimination.

I have a dream,
That all religions will never fight over who they are.

I have a dream,
That everyone will be together.

I have a dream,
That everyone will live in harmony.

Alex Baggott (13)
The High Arcal School, Dudley

My Mind

There's a weight on my mind
For years I have been resigned
But I know what must be done
All that I must be undone
But it's no fun when you're unkind
When you dig it makes me feel bad
Because to be big makes me sad
Do you think I want to be like this
I don't want to be like this anymore
But I feel like fighting a war
I can't help it, that's just the way it is
All I want is to find some kind of bliss
But all I seem to do is eat more
I'm trapped and need the key for the door
But I'm unique, and that's just me.

Victoria Fullford (13)
The High Arcal School, Dudley

Bullying . . .

Bullying
Is bad and wrong
Bullying
Is sad and uncalled for
Bullying
Will destroy people's lives
Bullying
Is not just physical
Bullying
Is always serious
Bullying
Can be mental
Bullying
Needs to be stopped!

Callum Andrews
The High Arcal School, Dudley

My Poem

I have a dream
When I wake up the world is bad.
I have a dream
That racism should never have been created.
I have a dream
Everyone should be treated the same
I have a dream
White people and black people are both equal.
I have a dream
Justice shall be done for racism
I have a dream
All people shall live in freedom
Praise the Lord
We are free at last
Hallelujah.

Ryan Bray (13)
The High Arcal School, Dudley

Children's Life . . .

Imagine . . .
Dark, empty silence.
Imagine . . .
Sitting in a room.
Imagine . . .
Having no one to talk to.
Imagine . . .
No food or water.
Imagine . . .
Being hit, bullied or tortured.
Imagine . . .
Don't sit there in silence.
Imagine . . .
If it was you!

Charlotte Collins-Farmer (13)
The High Arcal School, Dudley

228

Imagine

Imagine we respected the world we are living in
Thinking about our thoughts and actions towards our environment,
Thinking about the future
As our world should be a paradise.

Imagine living in an environment worth living in,
And stop adding to the problems we are already suffering.
Start being grateful as our world is getting disgraceful
As our world should be a paradise.

Imagine people started smiling,
If our world became a paradise
Our environment would be much safer.
Then finally people would be proud to live
Their lives in a place like no other.

Sophie Bram (13)
The High Arcal School, Dudley

The Hell Of Warfare

Gunshots surround me,
In a savage bloodbath,
Why can't it vanish?

A solider will fire,
Not knowing where bullets land,
Why can't it vanish?

In fields of hot blood,
A Hell where boys become men,
Why can't it vanish?

The uncertainty,
The fear of death floods me,
Why can't it vanish?

Connor Hutchinson (12)
The High Arcal School, Dudley

In That Field, I Dream . . .

In that field, that breathtaking meadow,
Filled with emerald grasslands which are bursting with crimson rubies
And indigo crystals that shimmer in the dazzling light
Of that immense solar disc in the sky, I lay.

I look up to the vast blue atmosphere above me,
I see the enormous cotton sheep which spiral gradually around my head.
I feel heat, rippling on my pale skin, but I still lay.

In this field, right now, my imagination goes insane,
Overflowing with thoughts and emotions.
I see many remarkable things in these clouds,
I feel like I am in a daydream which lasts for eternity.

I have a dream that one day, racism will be no more
And that no one is stereotypical towards others
And that anyone can walk the streets
Without the weight of prejudice on their shoulders.

I have a dream that one day, that there will be no war, just peace.
The threat of nuclear warfare has gusted away and died
Let's make every day Christmas Day, 1914 . . .

I dream one day that poverty will be over.
The citizens who roam the boulevards of Africa and Southern America,
Look up every day to the gigantic skyscrapers of Johannesburg or Rio
Towering over the tiny mud huts like bullies in a child's
Worst nightmare.

A plump drop of salty water runs down my blistered cheek
I sob as I see that cloud as black as coal rumbling angrily,
Ready to rain horror, terror and worry onto this world.
My imagination is as dark as that cloud,
I see a child, a young human, as scrawny as an old branch off an ancient
tree.
It's lime-green eyes, now as gloomy and as sour as a lemon.
Around it, a grim black ring, swollen and irritated
An empty expression looms on its face!
Its long, gaunt fingers held its thin legs and wailed into nothingness.
I ran, wiping the tears furiously away.
I dream, I thought, children be treated kindly, and with respect,
With no abuse.

I never go back to that field ever.
My mind torments me as I sit on my bench in that little park,
Nowhere else to go with my belongings at my side,
As I sob and howl piercingly, clasping my knees.
I never dare look at the sky now.
I see my past. That child. that face, so familiar . . .

Lauren Tolley (12)
Thomas Telford School, Telford

I Believe

I believe that all monkeys should be bright red,
I believe that elephants should be the same size as mice,
I believe that fish should eat sharks,
I believe that football should be played by all animals around the world.

I believe humans should be able to fly,
I believe we should be able to speak every language in the world,
I believe that we should need lemonade to stay alive, not water,
I believe that we should hit a golf ball a mile without it bouncing.

I believe everything in the world should cost nothing,
I believe that grass should be blue and the sky should be green,
I believe that the sun should rotate around the Earth,
I believe that leaves should be red.

I believe that chocolate is healthy,
I believe bananas are straight,
I believe pineapples are smooth,
I believe kiwis are spiky.

I believe PE should last for a whole day,
I believe humanities should be banned in all countries,
I believe ICT should only be computers,
I believe we should only go to school on weekends.

I know none of this is real.
But that is just what I believe.

Ben Harris (11)
Thomas Telford School, Telford

Sleepless Dream

When I sleep, I dream.
When I wake, I dream.
I dream that I am free.
But when I wake, I know that is not real.
The dream.

My life -
That's what's real.
The fight, the hate
The oppression the anger
The confusion, the hatred.
That's what's real.

My dream is for equality, freedom, justice, peace.
Freedom to be black.
Faith to be accepted.
Hope to be free.

My dream, oh my dream!
How I dream of better times.
A time not yet come
A time still to come
A time of my own
For my own
Not on my own.

Is it good to dream
To dare to dream
To have the right to dream?
Are dreamers doers
And are doers dreamers?
Because if I had the chance to do or dream
I would do.
I would do everything in my power to change things.
But I have no power.
I have no rights.

But I am right,
I know I am right
And right will overcome wrong
Good will overcome evil

And I will overcome my fate.
In my time,
In my way,
In my head,
In my dream.
My dream.

Thomas Aucott-Evans (12)
Thomas Telford School, Telford

Power

A gun for a battle, lost or won,
The vision of anger and power.
A flower so lost on her journey of life,
Where the voice is forgotten, now hidden away.

A whisper so soft,
Drifting around.
Heard through the world and felt through our hearts:
Resisting emotions, empowering the move,
Our spirits together, sharing the dream.

A mother with child, compassion and love
She whispers a song, so quiet and proud.
The crack of a gun, a life now lost,
Alone and so cold, the soul has gone.
She had a dream, now stolen away.

A voice on its own,
Battling along,
Struggling through life,
So proud and so strong.

So take the chance,
With the grasps of your hands,
For the dream you have,
Will come true one day.

James Hewlett (17)
Thomas Telford School, Telford

Change

All a *misunderestimated* joke,
not much caring for those Middle-Eastern folk.
They *must* be hiding WMDs
and so the eagle soared in with ease.

Free.

To do whatever it felt,
led by a Texan who wrongly spelt
the very words of the decree
that proclaimed all men are free.

Not just Americans, but *all men*,
spread throughout the Venn
diagram of gender, creed and race,
too often judged on their colour of face.

Fifty years ago, Parks and King fought
for a mighty cause that they thought
and believed would change the land.
Now one man has the right to stand.

She chose to sit and he to rise
to encourage others to realise
their own potential and dreams within.
He aims to change the world – not *win*.

Doubters defying the United State
patiently lie still and wait,
ready to jump on an error or flaw,
Failing to notice: he's won the war.

President of the USA,
ending Republican outlived stay.
As good as dead, the old regime,
replaced by Martin Luther's dream.

Daniel Yeo (18)
Thomas Telford School, Telford

I Have A Dream

I have a dream
That life will be worth living once again;
That we will wave a glad goodbye to pain –
I have a dream.

I have a dream
That one day soon we will not live in fear;
That the air will be healthy, fresh and clear –
I have a dream.

I have a dream
That justice will be won for all at last;
The world will understand that past is past;
I have a dream.

I have a dream
That each of us can share what we believe;
That everyone can offer and receive;
I have a dream.

I have a dream
That someday all our trading will be fair;
That hope will light the shadow of despair –
I have a dream.

I have a dream
That people will not mind that I am me;
That children can be who they want to be;
That at last we'll all live in unity.
I have a dream.

Emily Oldham (13)
Thomas Telford School, Telford

I Have A Dream

I am 100 years old, and I'm very nearly bald
But that's got nothing to do with you
I'm just a little old woman
Who just sits and summons
For people to listen to my dreams today
You see, I have a dream
That the guns will stop shooting
And that soon they'll just fade away
I have a dream
That the knives will stop stabbing
So that they won't come back again
I have a dream
That cigarettes will stop damaging
And soon they'll just smoke away
I have a dream
That the drugs will stop selling
And soon they'll just give away
So I have a dream
That these will stop killing
So that they'll just vanish today!

Riya Jutla (12)
Thomas Telford School, Telford

I Have A Dream . . .

I have a dream that school was one minute long
So kids can go out a lot more
I have a dream that we have soft chairs to sit on
So our bums don't hurt
I have a dream that schools have an ice rink
Tennis courts and sports complex
I have a dream that you can sit next to anyone in class
Not have a seating plan,

But my main dream is that we have no homework!

Sarah Rixom (12)
Thomas Telford School, Telford

I Have A Dream

I have a dream
Not an ordinary dream
I'm sure you have some too
But I just know that mine will come true.

Wolves are no longer a second flight team
It really is quite mean because
They're too good for the Championship
But not good enough for the Premier League.

One season we're up, the next we're down
That yo-yo really makes me frown
But one thing that makes me glad . . .
Is when the Old Gold score, I just go mad.

I have a dream that Wolves will win the title
I have a dream we'll stay in the Premier League.

I had a dream we'd get promoted,
I saw every game, I'm that devoted.
My dream is now we will succeed
And not drop out the Premier League.

Daniel Smith (12)
Thomas Telford School, Telford

I Have A Dream!

I have a dream that school ended at 12
And there would be no violence.

I have a dream that there should be no wars
And no racism in the world.

I have a dream that everyone should be treated the same
And people should get the same amount of food every day.

I have a dream today!

Leon Rogers
Thomas Telford School, Telford

I Have A Dream

I have a dream that I could win the NDPs
(National Development Plan)
I have a dream, that I got a perfect;
Floor
Rings
Vault
Parallel bars
High bar routine.

I have a dream, when I go to the trials for the national squad for gymnastics
They said I was good enough.

I have a dream that I am competing in European
and International competitions

I have a dream that when I get older I will be in the Commonwealth
Games and win!

I have a dream that I go to the Olympic games and win a gold medal
See my fans cheering and shouting my name.

I have a dream to help others make their dream become a reality.

Benji Howells (12)
Thomas Telford School, Telford

I Have A Dream

I have a dream that the world is made of chocolate
I have a dream that all chocolates are equal
No matter how small or large
Whether they are dark or milk
I have a dream that all chocolate should be counted
No matter what their imperfections or shapes are
I have a dream
            Do you?

Emily Cooper (11)
Thomas Telford School, Telford

238

I Have A Dream

I have a dream that all men should have a choice,
That choice is for freedom

I have a dream that no human should be harmed
For being a black citizen or foreign

I have a dream that all families should love
And cherish each other

I have a dream that war will end and peace will
Triumph in our world

I have a dream that all people should have a choice
For freedom and democracy

I have many dreams,
But there are two dreams I have forgotten
They are that . . .
The homeless will have homes and food and love
And that Barack Obama will bring peace to our beautiful planet.

I have a dream today!

Kieran Devereux (11)
Thomas Telford School, Telford

Imagination

Imagine a world where everyone's equal,
Violence and hate are all things of the past,
Going for gold and no one to hold you back,
Where you're free to think how you want to think,
Free to feel how you want to feel,
Let your imagination run wild,
Imagine a world where everyone's equal,
Violence and hate all things on the past.

Rashae Peart (12)
Thomas Telford School, Telford

I Have A Dream

I have a dream
That one day
We will all work together and laws we'll always obey

I have a dream
To say words that would mean kind
And cruelty we would leave behind

I have a dream
To start the day at ten o'clock and finish at one
Then go home and the day would soon be done.

I have a dream
To work hard, and have some fun
To be happy and joyful and shine like the sun

I have a dream
This day would never end
My love to the world I would like to send
And everybody would be my friend.

Nicola Maybury (11)
Thomas Telford School, Telford

I Have A Dream

I have a dream the only lesson in school day is PE
I have a dream you did whatever you wanted
I have a dream your dinner break was as long as you wanted it to be
I also have another dream that there were no exams.
What's your dream?

Jack Forrester (12)
Thomas Telford School, Telford

I Have A Dream

I have a dream
That I could scream
From my heart's content, I mean really extreme.

I have a dream
That I could be seen
From America, New Zealand, maybe even Beijing.

I have a dream
Of my favourite ice cream
Five storeys high with strawberry cream.

I have a dream
Of a romantic stream
With ducks and fish in a sunset scene.

I have a dream
That none of these things were a dream
They would all come to life, it would be supreme.

Charlotte Dyke (12)
Thomas Telford School, Telford

I Have A Dream . . .

I have a dream that there was clean water
For everyone and it was never polluted.

I have a dream that people could always be treated
With good medicine so they can become well and not die.

I have a dream that people could travel
All around the world without spending all of their money.

I have a dream that people could get jobs
And earn enough for their families.

I have a dream that forests would never be cut down
And the animals could live their lives without disturbance.

I have a dream today!

Tim Smith (12)
Thomas Telford School, Telford

I Have A Dream

I have a dream that
I can touch the sky
I can walk on water
And I can fly!

You have a dream that
You can run faster than light
Live on Mars and
Get everything right.

We have a dream that
We can live for hundreds of years
Dance when we're 90 and
Talk to all of our peers.

Now, a dream is a dream
And anything can happen
As long as you believe.

Amy Hunt (12)
Thomas Telford School, Telford

I Have A Dream

I have a dream that school would be fun and games,
So that we wouldn't get bored,
I have a dream that everyone would be judged the same,
Not by age or skin colour,
I have a dream that there was no cruelty in the world,
I have a dream that some day all animals will be treated well,
I have a dream that poverty did not exist,
I have a dream that everything was free,
I have a dream everyone had food on a plate morning and night,
I have a dream that everyone has a cosy, warm and safe place to sleep,
I have a dream that everyone could not be ill,
That is my dream
One day I hope my dream will be true.

Sam Murdoch (12)
Thomas Telford School, Telford

My Dream

I put my pads and helmet on, I am going in to bat;
The bowler marks his run up;
I prepare to face his ball.

Just three to draw and four to win, my nervous friends all shout;
The bowler bowls, it's at the stumps.
I take a mighty swipe.

The ball flies up into the air;
'Catch it! Catch it! the fielders call, but nobody replies;
Rising, Rising up away into the sky.

I see the umpire's finger lift, my heart begins to sink;
But then another finger, it's a six I think.
'We've won! We've won!' shout the others in my team;
And I am the hero of this game, at least for now it seems.

Or was it only in my dream?

Ryan Ball (11)
Thomas Telford School, Telford

My Poem

I have a dream that the moon is made of cheese
And the is no such thing as fleas,
We all live on the planet Mars
Eating Galaxys, Milky Ways and Mars bars.

I have a dream that there are no animals and fishy cods
And we all travel in vehicles that look like pea pods,
We all have our own rockets
There are no cough sweets called Lockets.

I have a dream that we drink sprout juice – yuck!
So that's why everybody's green - a nice look!
Now that's the end of my dream! Let it shine!
Hope yours is nicer than mine.

Katie Beech (12)
Thomas Telford School, Telford

243

I Have A Wonderful Dream

I wish every day there was peace in the world

H elpful people will always go far in life
A small idea and a big idea are both equal
V endettas shouldn't be used, always say sorry and make up
E veryone should have an equal chance in life.

A n adventure is all you need to have in life

D rive yourself on to overcome your fears
R eady at all times that's what you should be
E nergy, determination and strength makes a successful person
A happy person will get through the day with no problem
M y favourite expression is always stand up for yourself.

James Mackie (12)
Thomas Telford School, Telford